ACHIEVING
EYPS

Leading Practice in Early Years Settings

Mary E. Whalley

Series editors: Lyn Trodd and Gill Goodliff

LearningMatters

First published in 2008 by Learning Matters Ltd

British Library Cataloguing in Publication Data
A CIP record for this book is available from the British Library.

ISBN: 978 1 84445 176 0

UNIVERSITY OF CHICHESTER

Cover design by Phil Barker
Text design by Code 5 Design Associates Ltd
Project management by Swales & Willis
Typeset by Swales & Willis Ltd, Exeter, Devon
Printed and bound in Great Britain by TJ International Ltd, Padstow, Cornwall

Learning Matters Ltd
33 Southernhay East
Exeter EX1 1 NX
Tel: 01392 215560
info@learningmatters.co.uk
www.learningmatters.co.uk

FSC
Mixed Sources
Product group from well-managed
forests and other controlled sources
Cert no. SGS-COC-2482
www.fsc.org
© 1996 Forest Stewardship Council

Dedication

This book is dedicated to the memory of my daughter,
Anna Whalley-Moutter (1976–2005) who herself was a dedicated
professional, committed always to 'best practice' in everything she
did, including sharing teaching and learning with young children.

Contents

List of figures

List of tables

Foreword from the series editor

This book is one of a series which will be of interest to all those following pathways towards achieving Early Years Professional Status (EYPS). This includes students on Sector-Endorsed Early Years Foundation Degree programmes and undergraduate Early Childhood Studies degree courses as these awards are key routes towards EYPS.

The graduate EYP role was developed as a key strategy in government commitment to improve the quality of Early Years care and education in England, especially in the private, voluntary and independent sectors. Policy documents and legislation such as *'Every Child Matters: Change for Children'* DfES (2004); the *'Ten Year Childcare Strategy: Choice for Parents – the Best Start for Children'* HMT (2004) and the Childcare Act, 2006, identified the need for high-quality, well-trained and educated professionals to work with the youngest children. At the time of writing (May 2008), the Government's aim is to have Early Years Professionals (EYPs) in all Children's Centres by 2010 and in every full day care setting by 2015.

Each book in the series focuses on underpinning aspects of the EYP role. To support the professional development towards achieving EYPS the contents foreground links to the EYP Standards.

This book is a significant contribution to the extensive, general discourse of leadership and in particular to understandings of leading practice in the early years. Mary E. Whalley, with Shirley Allen and Dilys Wilson, develop important new thinking about *leadership of practice* in Early Years settings. They discuss and explore the theme in diverse contexts reflecting the range of professional backgrounds of EYPs. Throughout the book authentic case studies and reflective tasks are used to deepen readers' learning. The final chapter looks at professional development beyond the achievement of Early Years Professional Status and considers how such development can refine and re-define leadership of practice.

Leadership of practice by EYPs is intended to promote high quality experiences for children under the age of five. *Leading Practice in Early Years Settings* greatly extends our understanding of this key feature of the EYP role and we are delighted to commend it to you.

Gill Goodliff and Lyn Trodd
May 2008

About the authors and series editors

Shirley Allen

Shirley Allen is a Senior Lecturer in Early Childhood Studies at Middlesex University. In this role, she is co-leader of the Early Years Professional Status programme and a tutor on the Early Childhood Studies Degree. She has previously worked in teacher education on undergraduate and PGCE programmes at the University of Hertfordshire. A former primary school teacher, she taught for a number of years in London schools and was a deputy head of an infant school. Her research interests are in the areas of mentoring, outdoor play and children's literacy development in the Early Years.

Gill Goodliff

Gill Goodliff is a Lecturer in Early Years at the Open University where she teaches on work-based learning courses in the Sector-Endorsed Foundation Degree in Early Years and is a Lead Assessor for Early Years Professional Status. Her professional background with young children and their families was predominantly in the Public Voluntary and Independent sector. Her current research focuses on the professional development and identities of Early Years practitioners and young children's spirituality.

Lyn Trodd

Lyn Trodd is a Principal Lecturer and Head of Children's Workforce Development at the University of Hertfordshire. She is currently Chair of the Sector-Endorsed Foundation Degree in Early Years national network. Lyn was a member of Children's Workforce Development Council reference group consulted about the new status for Early Years Professionals and led a team which piloted EYPS at the University of Hertfordshire. Her research is focused on graduate roles for members of the Children Workforce and how professional learning programmes develop self-efficacy in participants.

Mary E. Whalley

Mary Whalley is a Lecturer in Early Years at Leeds Metropolitan University, primarily involved in HE within FE provision in the delivery of the Sector Endorsed Early Years Foundation Degree. She also works for Leeds Metropolitan University and Best Practice on the Early Years Professional Status programme. A former primary school teacher, she taught for a number of years in the Early Years department of a special school before becoming a Teacher Fellow at Manchester University, exploring effective pedagogy for young children with special educational needs. Her research interests are in the areas of work-based learning within higher education, children's creativity and play-based learning.

Dilys Wilson

Dilys Wilson is based at Middlesex University as a senior lecturer in Early Childhood Studies and co-leader for the Early Years Professional Status programme. For many years she was involved in Early Years NVQ training and assessing in a College of Further Education. Prior to that, she worked as a teacher in a range of settings with children aged between two and six years. She has a special interest in integrated care and education and in the contribution of childminders to the Early Years workforce. Her research interests are based around children's emotional experiences and the role of adults in supporting children's social and emotional development.

Acknowledgements

This is an exciting time to be involved in the Early Years Professional Status programme which is, without a doubt, 'good news' for Early Years practitioners, children and their families. It has been both an enormous privilege and a huge responsibility to have prepared this book. It has been a partnership venture and I must record my thanks to a number of individuals, without whom this book would not have been written.

Firstly, my sincere thanks to Shirley Allen and Dilys Wilson of Middlesex University. Shirley has written Chapter 7 and co-written Chapter 5 with Dilys. They both bring considerable expertise to their writing and the way they have 'unpacked' the task of the Early Years Professional in leading delivery of the Early Years Foundation Stage in Chapter 5 is quite remarkable, given the short time between the publication of the Early Years Foundation Stage framework and the deadline for this book. I am very grateful to them, too, for their helpful feedback on my own writing. Patsi Noakes, a former colleague at Leeds Metropolitan University and trusted friend, gave me significant support in writing Chapter 3 on equality practice, as did Liz Leatherbarrow, Early Years Advisory Teacher for North Yorkshire. I record my heartfelt thanks to them both.

The book is punctuated with case studies and here I record my special thanks to a number of Early Years Professionals with whom I have worked personally and to others, especially through Leeds Metropolitan University, the Best Practice Network and Middlesex University, who responded to my requests for their reflections on their roles as leaders of practice. I have been able to use all the material these wonderful people provided and wish them all well as they enjoy their new status and continue on their own learning journeys. My colleagues at Leeds Metropolitan University have been very supportive, too, allowing for my preoccupation with writing and making encouraging sounds when I have met with them.

My deep thanks must be recorded to Lyn Trodd and Gill Goodliff, the series editors, who had the original ideas for this book and others relating to Early Years Professional Status. I thank them both for the initial confidence they showed in me to begin writing in the first place and for their constant encouragement throughout. Lyn, in particular, has been inspirational in her feedback and a true 'critical friend'. The publisher, Julia Morris and development editor, Jennifer Clark have been consistently helpful and responsive through all stages of writing and I thank them sincerely, too.

Finally, my profound gratitude goes to my husband, Ernie, daughters, Sara and Rachel, and grandchildren, Nia and James, who have given me their unstinting support, endured my distractedness and surrounded me with their love and care as I focused on the writing. I have appreciated this more than I can express.

Mary E. Whalley

1   Leadership of practice: towards a new understanding

CHAPTER OBJECTIVES

This chapter provides a rationale for the book and offers some definitions of 'leadership' and 'management' in an Early Years context. The concept of the Early Years Professional is considered in the light of the European model of 'social pedagogue' and pedagogical leadership. Key characteristics of a leader as a supportive and interactive role model and instigator of change are outlined and a tentative definition of 'leader of practice' is offered. Reflective tasks, case studies and self-assessment activities are included in the chapter so that you can begin to explore your role as a leader of the practice of others and gather the evidence of this role that you will need in order to achieve Early Years Professional Status.

After reading this chapter you should be able to:
- reflect on the concept of leadership in Early Years practice;
- appraise critically the role of the pedagogue and its potential as a model for the leader of practice;
- begin to apply an appropriate understanding of leadership of practice to your own role as you prepare to meet the Standards for Early Years Professionals.

This chapter is wide-ranging and will help you to reflect on how you influence and lead the practice of others in relation to most of the Standards for Early Years Professionals.

Introduction

As the first Early Years Professionals (EYPs) reach the point of validation and are awarded Early Years Professional Status, many different examples of leadership of practice are emerging. These illustrate the diverse facets of the role. However, a more specific definition of leadership in the context of Early Years practice would seem to be needed that captures the essence of leadership of practice. Even within the *Children's Workforce Strategy* (DfES, 2006a: 29), the references to the new 'strategic leadership role . . . and the core skills, knowledge and values' that go with it seem to sit more comfortably with the models illustrated through the National Professional Qualification for (school) Headships (NPQH) and the National Professional Qualification for Integrated Centre Leadership (NPQICL). Whilst these offer valid pathways for leadership development and training, for those who are leading **organisations,** they are not the models that best fit the need for a clear definition of leadership of **practice**. Indeed, the juxtaposition of the developing Children's Centre agenda with the emergence of Early Years Professional Status (EYPS) is creating a situation where urgent clarification is needed between the two distinct types of leadership.

The emergence of the role of Early Years Professional is fundamental to the Government's agenda to improve workforce skills, knowledge and competencies and to raise the quality of children's experiences in the Early Years (Children's Workforce Development Council [CWDC], 2007a). Candidates seeking validation for EYPS not only have to demonstrate that they can meet the 39 Standards 'through their own practice' they also have to provide evidence that they can 'lead and support others' to do so (CWDC, 2007a).

It is this 'leadership *of practice*' as a defining element – indeed one of the three core skills – of the EYP role (CWDC, 2007b), which is the focus of this book. In this chapter, we explore definitions of leadership and how these differ from 'management' of a setting. How distinctive is 'leadership of practice' and can we find an appropriate definition for it? Does the role of pedagogue developed in many European countries offer any insights here?

What is leadership?

Leadership is a complex subject that is often misunderstood (Horne and Stedman Jones, 2001). Almost two decades ago, Cuban (1988: 190) conducted research into leadership in schools and concluded that there are 'more than 350 definitions of leadership, but no clear and unequivocal understanding as to what distinguishes *leaders* from *non-leaders*'. If anything, the situation is even more complex today, with a diverse range of settings catering for the needs of children. However, 'leadership' is a term that is applied within many professions and most organisations and, from the outset, it is important to attempt to distinguish 'leadership' from 'management'. Confusingly, the two terms are often used interchangeably and distinctive definitions are hard to establish, especially as they are often linked in Early Years practice. Indeed some theorists (Hall, 1996) have argued that research shows it is unethical to separate leadership from management:

> *Leadership is a philosophy in action and management is an integral part. The women heads (in the study) were therefore simultaneously leaders and managers. Managing without leadership was unethical; leadership without management was irresponsible.*
> (Hall, 1996: 11)

The leadership element of the EYP role, however, does not inherently link together leadership with management. Whilst acknowledging the usefulness to the role of some management *skills,* the EYP is essentially to be a leader of high quality practice.

What do you understand by the terms 'leadership' and 'management'?

- *How different are the two concepts/roles in your experience?*

- *Think of experiences when you were well-led, or well-managed. How did you know that your leader/manager was doing a good job?*

- *Have there been times when you felt you were experiencing poor or inadequate leadership or management?*

- *Can you begin to identify factors that influenced your experience?*

Law and Glover (2000, cited in Rodd, 2006) offer helpful insights into the different emphases of the two roles.

Table 1.1 Managers and leaders

Managers:	Leaders:
Plan and make decisions	Give direction
Organise and clarify work	Offer inspiration
Coordinate the organisation	Build teamwork
Control and monitor the organisation's effectiveness	Set an example
	Gain respect and acceptance

(Rodd, 2006: 20)

Leadership in the Early Years

A more detailed review of the available literature on leadership in the Early Years is offered in the next chapter. However, in seeking to establish a new understanding of a leader of practice it is important to consider here the perspectives of some of the key writers on leadership in the Early Years as you seek to clarify your own role in leading practice.

Solley (2003), from her position of nursery headteacher, suggests that the distinctive difference between leadership and management is quite clear: management involves *maintenance and oversight* of an organisation, whereas leadership is more to do with *enhancement, improvement and development*. This implies that leadership and management 'complement each other' (Smith and Langston, 1999: 6). However, the focus for the new role of EYP foregrounds leadership.

Leadership of practice

Moyles (2006) believes that concepts of leadership and management have yet to be fully explored in an Early Years context. Indeed, you have a key role in this, as your emergent roles as Early Years Professionals are helping to shape our understanding of leadership. Although discussing mainly leadership of an organisation, rather than of *practice*, one of the difficulties Moyles identifies is that of finding an appropriate title for the 'head' of an Early Years setting. In some, especially in the private sector, the head is usually described as a 'manager'. In the voluntary sector, she is a 'leader' or 'supervisor'. In a children's centre, there is a leader/manager – who may well have completed the National Professional Qualification for Integrated Centre Leadership (NPQICL) – and may also be an Early Years 'teacher' who has **not** completed the NPQICL but is usually viewed as the leader of practice. In many settings – particularly in the private, voluntary and independent sector, the leader and manager are the same person. Are you confused? Little wonder!

CASE STUDY

Leadership and management

Andrea, EYP: '*In the course of 15 years, I have worked as a teacher in a Reception class, a supervisor in a voluntary pre-school and as a registered childminder in my own home. I have had significant experience of working with children within the birth to five age range and last year became the coordinator for the local childminding network, organising professional development and training events for childminders. In most of the roles I have held, I believe there have been aspects of both leadership and management. In my present role, I make sure all runs smoothly in the network, just as I did as a teacher in school and as pre-school supervisor. These are 'management' tasks. But I also see it important to be innovative and plan for change and this requires 'leadership' skills.*'

Reflecting on the different roles she has held over the years, Andrea is able to identify the key aspects of her role where she is leader and an initiator of change. However, not all EYPs are able to recognise opportunities for leadership quite so clearly. Use the following task to identify, within your context and setting, the opportunities you have to lead and improve practice.

PRACTICAL TASK

Finding evidence of leadership of practice

1. *Take a piece of paper and divide it into four equal parts and then further divide these sections into 2 columns.*

2. *Each of the four parts will represent different aspects of your role: your work with children; your work within a team of practitioners; your work in partnership with parents and carers; and your work with other professionals (see Figure 1.1).*

3 *In the first column of each section identify where you recognise you are already demonstrating leadership of practice and initiating change. In the second column, try to identify further opportunities to develop this.*

Work with children		Work with parents and carers	
Now ?	Further opportunities	Now ?	Further opportunities
Work within staff team		Work with other professionals	
Now ?	Further opportunities	Now ?	Further opportunities

Figure 1.1 Working with others

This exercise offers you a strong reminder that EYPs do not operate in isolation. The EYP Standards themselves are grouped to demonstrate the collaborative and interactive nature of the role, for instance S25–28 relate to interaction with children, S33–36 to teamwork and collaboration, and so on. *Who* you are 'leading' will impact on *how* you lead. Although set in the context of NPQICL, Margy Whalley (2005a: 7) defines this as a 'community development approach', with the setting viewed as a 'learning community' which recognises the inter-relatedness of the children, families, staff and wider community. Within the learning community, the leader has the opportunity to address the following elements:

- developing the individual's capacity to be self-directing;
- helping individuals to gain more control over their lives;
- raising self-esteem;
- promoting learning as a life-long learning experience;
- equality of opportunity;
- pushing boundaries;
- 'constructive discontent' – not having to put up with things because it's 'just the way they are';

- encouraging people to feel they have the power and confidence to change things;
- self-fulfilment (Whalley, 2005a).

REFLECTIVE TASK

- *Are there similarities between this list and yours?*
- *What do you make of the notion of 'constructive discontent' as a trigger for change? Are you able to identify an example from your own practice where collectively staff identified and worked together to effect change?*

Within the 'learning community', then, each member of the staff team needs be involved in contributing to change in practice. One very important aspect of the role of the leader of practice here is to model a positive disposition to change, demonstrating a clear 'hands-on' approach and showing others what is possible in the development and enhancement of practice. We might call this 'visible leadership', which is dependent on effective engagement between the leader and other staff. Think here of Albert Bandura's social learning theory (1977) which suggests that children will (unconsciously) model their own behaviour on those with whom they have a close and trusting relationship. This can be applied to your role as EYP, too. Remember that whilst most people within your sphere of influence will – consciously and unconsciously – take note of what you *do*, those with whom you have forged a positive relationship will also *imitate* your practice. This brings both privilege and responsibility.

REFLECTIVE TASK

Take a few moments to think about some of those significant to your own professional formation and development and who have influenced you.

- *In what ways do you believe they modelled effective practice and you imitated this?*
- *How might you use these reflections to enhance your own opportunities as a role model within your own leadership of practice?*

Towards a definition of leadership of practice

By now you should be developing a clearer awareness of how the existing models and concepts of leadership do not quite fit what is needed for the Early Years Professional role. However, Rodd (2006) offers helpful insights in her description of leadership as a 'holistic, inclusive and empowering process'. This reminds us of the interactive behaviour of leaders of practice, where a sense of community is established, all feel valued, respected and included, and diversity is embraced.

- **Vision behaviour:** envisioning change and taking risks to bring it about.

- **Values behaviour:** building trust and openness.

- **People behaviour:** building caring relationships, with respect for individual differences.

- **Influence behaviour:** the capacity to work collaboratively. (Adapted from Rodd, 2006: 33)

This emphasis on leadership as a range of *behaviours* further reinforces the importance of modelling high quality practice.

> **REFLECTIVE TASK**
>
> *Look particularly at S25, 30, 33, 34, 35, 36 and 39. Using a similar grid to that suggested on page 5, write down the opportunities you have to demonstrate these leadership behaviours in the context of each of these Standards. Reflect on further opportunities you might develop here.*

Leadership qualities

Moyles (2006) has defined the Effective Leadership and Management Scheme – Early Years (ELMS–EY) using the metaphor of a tree with four distinct branches: leadership qualities; management skills; professional attributes; and personal characteristics and attitudes. The ELMS–EY model is essentially a tool by which practitioners who lead/manage Early Years settings can evaluate their own effectiveness and is particularly appropriate for those following the NPQICL route. It is notable, however, that Moyles does differentiate here

between leadership qualities and management skills; and the leadership qualities' 'branch' (complete with 'stem' and 'leaves') of the ELMS-EY nonetheless offers very helpful indicators of leadership which can be applied specifically to leadership of practice.

You may find Moyles' characteristics of effective Early Years leadership helpful as you reflect on your own role: In what ways are you:

- visionary?

- responsible for and thoughtful about basic needs: of children, staff families and setting?

- accountable for quality?

- charismatic, with integrity, engaging others, commanding and offering respect and motivating staff?

- flexible and versatile?

- knowledgeable and an informational resource for the staff?

- aware of the importance of shared values?

- able to lead and manage change?

- empower and enable all relevant people?

- a culture setter?

(Adapted from Moyles, 2006: 21–22)

Effective leadership of practice

Without doubt, the work of Siraj-Blatchford, with others, has been influential in shaping our understanding of leadership in the Early Years (Siraj-Blatchford et al., 2002; Sylva et al., 2004). Most recently, Siraj-Blatchford has collaborated with Manni (2007) on researching effective leadership in the Early Years sector (the ELEYS study). Their aim was to identify the characteristics or patterns of leadership that can be identified in settings judged to be offering the highest quality early learning experiences for children and families. Here is a rigorous approach to determining just what kind of leaders – and leadership skills – contribute to the best practice in Early Years provision. Although the ELEYS study adopts a much broader understanding of leadership than the one emerging as appropriate for the leader of practice, there are insights here that help shape our emerging definition of EYP leadership, especially the notion of 'building a learning community and team culture' (Siraj-Blatchford and Manni, 2007: 21). This concept of 'continuous engagement with staff in professional practice' is also one of the key elements identified as part of the NPQICL role of 'pedagogical leadership' (Whitaker, 2004: 8) The parallels between the EYP role and that of pedagogue in many European countries are explored a little later in the chapter.

Leadership of practice in a variety of settings

The model of leadership of practice required for EYPS is one that must fit across all types of Early Years settings and sit equally comfortably in a home setting, a voluntary pre-school in a small village hall, a private nursery or a large children's centre. We are seeking to define a new model or paradigm of leadership which best fits Early Years Professional Status and which is, in part, being informed and shaped by EYPs themselves as they bring to the role a wide range of professional experience and qualifications. Common ground is found when each of you takes the opportunity to reflect on your own strengths and to identify appropriate and often innovative ways of demonstrating leadership by inspiring others.

Early Years Professionals are indeed a diverse group of people, drawn from different professional backgrounds, working in a range of settings: maintained, private, voluntary and independent. The role of EYP is an aspirational one, in which the EYP seeks to demonstrate and model the highest possible commitment to quality Early Years practice and to lead and improve the practice of others across the Early Years Foundation Stage (EYFS). However, it is important to remember that each of you will select ways to offer the EYP Standards from the perspective of your own professional context.

Consider some EYP candidates here:

Sally *is an experienced Early Years teacher who spent six years as deputy head of a primary school while managing Foundation Stage provision. She now works as the teacher in a children's centre as part of the senior management team with the centre manager and the room supervisors of the baby, toddler and pre-school rooms.*

Aliya *has a background in social work but for the past three years has been employed as team member of a Sure Start Local Project in a culturally diverse urban area. Her work includes twice-weekly toy library sessions, and leading lunchtime parent and toddler sessions and crèche provision while parents attend English or Computing Skills classes.*

Joe *is room leader in a private nursery and had the opportunity to complete a Sector Endorsed Foundation Degree Early Years and then 'top-up' to a BA (Hons) Childhood Studies while he continued to work. Three colleagues work with Joe in the pre-school room which caters for up to 20 children at any one session.*

Debbie *is a graduate nurse, with previous experience of working in a private nursery setting, who is currently working as the childminder of a baby of eight months, a three-year-old boy and a four-year-old girl. Her close friend, Anna, is also a childminder in the locality and Debbie and Anna meet regularly together and bring their charges. Anna has only just started her Early Years training and often asks Debbie for advice about her practice.*

REFLECTIVE TASK

Try not to focus on the obvious differences in each of these cases. Instead, can you identify anything that these EYPs have in common in the way they are demonstrating leadership of practice?

Consider again the contexts of these EYPs and then reflect on your own. Are you able to identify further examples of evidence of your own skills in leading others' practice?

The pedagogue role

Who are you calling a pedagogue?

(Jackson, 2005)

When the CWDC first produced its draft proposals for the new professional status in the developing children's workforce (CWDC, 2005) two possible titles were mooted:

- **New teacher** – signifying a specialist Early Years teacher qualification similar to that in operation in New Zealand and Spain.

- **Social pedagogue** – drawing specifically on the Danish model of Early Years graduate professionals. Across Denmark it is social pedagogues who are the main workers in nurseries and other children's settings. Other continental European countries operate a similar system, with a shared understanding of the role, though in some the role is known simply as the 'pedagogue'. Some countries also include working with teenagers and adults as part of the social pedagogue role.

For a wide range of reasons, following consultation on the draft proposals, both these terms were rejected in favour of 'Early Years Professional'. However, it is worth a closer look at the concept of the social pedagogue and the insights this may offer into the distinctiveness of the EYP role.

The role of the 'pedagogue' has its roots in nineteenth-century Germany and was developed in response to what has been termed 'schoolification', where the teacher is viewed as a 'technician' within a 'regime of performativity' (Ranson et al., 2004, cited in Petrie, 2005). This view assumes there is a bank of knowledge and skills to be acquired by a child and the educator's role is mainly to impart these within set targets and time frameworks. This is often referred to as the 'transmission' code of learning (Bottery, 1990) where the child is a '*passive* recipient' and teacher/educator's role is that of '*active* transmitter' of knowledge. Such a model does not fit easily in an Early Years context where children are seen as developing in different ways and at different rates (DCSF, 2008a) and the adult role one of 'supporting children's learning within an enabling, facilitating and observing role rather than directly as 'teachers'' (Moyles et al., 2002). Part of the definition of the pedagogue emphasises the relationship with the child as a whole being, supporting all aspects of the child's development equally and working with each child to establish positive dispositions for learning.

> *The pedagogue sets out to address the whole child, the child with body, mind motions, creativity, history and social identity. This is not the child only of emotions – the psycho-therapeutic approach, nor only of the body – the medical approach, nor only of the mind – the traditional teaching approach.*

(Moss and Petrie, 2002)

The concept of the pedagogue is intrinsically linked to an understanding of Early Years pedagogy. This is an extremely complex phenomenon and the findings from the Study of Pedagogical Effectiveness in Early Learning (SPEEL) suggest that it includes 'both the behaviour of teaching and being able to talk about and reflect on teaching; it encompasses both what practitioners actually *do* and *think* and the principles, theories, perceptions and challenges that inform and shape these.' (Moyles et al., 2002:12). The findings from the SPEEL project (Moyles et al., 2007) have been influential in the development of EYPS. So, applying this here to the EYP role as that of pedagogical leader, we can see that s/he is a highly qualified reflective practitioner, able to draw on a breadth of experience to articulate and demonstrate both a principled value stance to and strong in-depth knowledge and understanding of the learning and developmental needs of children from birth to five. Your evidence from EYP Standards 1–6 will need to show these aspects of your role and how you lead the practice of others.

This view of the pedagogue role and Early Years pedagogy therefore offers us a very clearly defined pattern of Early Years provision which is quite deliberately and robustly different from the school experience (Payler, 2005). Research by the British Educational Research Association Early Years Special Interest Group (BERA, 2003) suggested that pedagogical processes in the Early Years are most evident in the child's development of a sense of self and becoming sociable, in play activities (Moyles, 2005: 8 refers to 'playful pedagogy') and through the interactive nature of learning between child and adult, especially in the way that this results in shared meanings. As these processes are all central to the role of the EYP, we can begin to conclude that the concept of pedagogical leadership is one that accords with EYPS.

Boddy et al. (2005: 3) develop further understanding of the pedagogue role, describing it as one of 'strategic leadership', particularly in being reflective and applying self-knowledge to practice; being practical and creative; exercising teamwork based on dialogue, democratic practice and valuing the contribution of others; and in managing change. You may feel unfamiliar with the terminology linked to the pedagogue role but you have now had the opportunity to consider some of the characteristics that help define it and we hope you can see some compatibility with the EYP role.

CASE STUDY

Jennie, a lead practitioner in a children's centre, was able to visit an Early Years setting in Sweden as part of an exchange programme.

'Although the 'pedagogue' title sounded strange to my ears, I was struck with all the similarities between the role of the pedagogue in the Swedish early childhood centre and my own at home. My counterpart in the setting carried out her role in much the same way I do: she was totally passionate about the children and knew so much about each of them and their families. She was committed to play-based learning and to following the children's leads and interests in nurturing each aspect of development. I was struck by how much time the staff spent listening to children, really listening and, although I couldn't understand the Swedish language, I could tell from the children's responses that these interactive conversations were helping to develop children's thinking.'

REFLECTIVE TASK

Does Jennie's experience here help you to draw more parallels between the European model of the pedagogue and our own EYP? Jennie was struck with the quality of the conversations between adult and children. How do you see this linking to S15, 16 and 26? Is there anything else from the case study that supports your reflection on your own leadership role?

Leadership of change

The concluding aspect of strategic leadership outlined by Boddy et al (2005) is that of managing change. Given the rapid period of growth and transformation within Early Years practice and provision at the present time, the task of EYPs to 'act as agents of change' (CWDC, 2007a: 2) is a fundamental part of the rationale for the emergence of the role. The concept of the 'agent of change' is an interesting one. It has scientific roots in defining a catalyst or that which effects a behavioural change. Thus, the thinking behind this choice of phrase is that the EYP will intentionally or indirectly cause or accelerate changes to practice. Essentially, as an agent of change, you will need to have a high level of self-awareness, particularly in understanding your own reactions to change, and you will need emotional intelligence (Goleman, 1996). These are prerequisites to the more proactive aspects of the role as agent of change, which will include modelling appropriate behaviours and practices, sharing your knowledge and expertise with colleagues, engaging in dialogue with them, using imaginative ways of presenting new ideas and – through strong rapport – persuading them to come on board.

REFLECTIVE TASK

As you begin to explore your role as an agent of change, think about those five dimensions and see if you can identify examples from your own practice.

Table 1.2 Agents of change

Strategy for agent of change	Example from practice
Role-modelling appropriate behaviours and practices	
Sharing your knowledge and expertise	
Engaging in two-way dialogue with colleagues	
Imaginative and innovative ways to introduce change	
Persuasion	

CHAPTER SUMMARY

This books aims to support you as you prepare for the EYP validation process. In particular, it focuses on your role as leader of practice and agent of change. All of you, no matter what your route to EYPS or the type of setting you are in, should welcome the opportunity to reflect both on your own practice and on the way you lead and support others. The case studies of other EYPs or those aspiring to the role are offered in this book to help you to reflect on your own role. This emphasis on different aspects of the EYP role in leading practice is explored more fully in the remaining chapters but you will have noted a tentative definition emerging here at the outset. In being a leader of practice, you will demonstrate:

- reflective and reflexive practice in your own role;

- skills in decision-making;

- sound knowledge and understanding of Early Years pedagogy: the holistic needs of all children from birth to five and competence in planning, implementing and monitoring within the Early Years Foundation Stage framework (DCSF, 2008a);

- a strong sense of the intrinsic worth of each child and all those in her/his world;

- the ability to role-model, lead and support others in high quality practice;

- the ability to define a vision for practice within a setting;

- competence as an agent of change.

In this chapter we have focused mainly on the adult role as we have begun to explore some of the thinking that is informing the different models and understanding of leadership in Early Years at the current time. Despite the challenge of clear definition, there is growing understanding that the difference between leadership and management lies in the distinctive emphases of the roles: the manager maintains and ensures the smooth running of an organisation whereas the leader focuses on development and innovation (Solley, 2003). We have begun to identify clearly that in working towards EYP status, what is needed is a more focused understanding of leadership: that of leading and improving practice. In particular, the EYP needs to demonstrate specific skills in leading EYFS provision and in leading change effectively.

Moving on

In our opening discussion here on aspects of the EYP leadership role, we have identified some of the key writers on leadership in early childhood settings. In the next chapter, we engage in a review of this and other available literature on Early Years leadership. This will begin with a broad outline of some of the classic theories on leadership but will focus primarily on relevant research projects on leadership in Early Years contexts. Standards 1–6 require evidence of knowledge and understanding of principles, policy and practice. The EYP who is genuinely committed to the highest quality delivery will keep abreast of key research findings in order to consolidate, update and enhance his/her own knowledge and understanding.

PRACTICAL TASK

Table 1.3 is a series of statements made by Early Years practitioners when asked to define leadership. Please tick the judgement that most accurately fits your viewpoint.

- *Are there any statements with which you strongly agree?*

- *Are there any with which you strongly disagree?*

- *Your judgements are based to a large extent on your own professional values. Are you aware of how these have been shaped?*

Table 1.3 Defining leadership

An effective leader is:	Strongly agree	Agree	Neither agree nor disagree	Disagree	Strongly disagree
1. highly qualified					
2. someone who commands respect					
3. someone who is easy to relate to					
4. someone who models good practice					
5. able to identify creative solutions					
6. able to acknowledge her/his own vulnerabilities and mistakes					
7. skilled in conflict management					
8. able to relate to a wide range of people					
9. child-centred in her/his practice					
10. respecting and valuing of all members of the team					
11. able to steer change in practice					
12. able to delegate					

Self-assessment questions

1. What are the main differences between 'leadership' and 'management' as defined by Law and Glover? (Answer: page 3)

2. Why was the NPQICL developed? How is this route qualitatively different from that taken by EYPS candidates? (Answer: pages 1–2, 5)

3. Name the four aspects of leadership 'behaviour' that Rodd (2006) has identified. (Answer: page 7)

4. What are the four 'branches' of Moyles' (2006) Effective Management and Leadership Scheme? (Answer: page 7)

5. In what ways does the Early Years Professional role mirror the European model of 'social pedagogue'? (Answer – see definition on page 10)

Moyles, J. (2006) The leadership qualities branch, Chapter 3 in *Effective Leadership and Management in the Early Years.* Maidenhead: Open University Press.

Rodd, J. (2006) Unpacking leadership in the early childhood context, Chapter 1 in *Leadership in Early Childhood.* Maidenhead: Open University Press.

2 Leadership in the Early Years: a review of the literature

CHAPTER OBJECTIVES

This chapter provides a review of current literature of leadership theories and research findings. Starting with broad reference to classic leadership theories, the focus will narrow to consider further the literature on leadership in the Early Years. Drawing on both UK-based and international research, including Scandinavia, the USA, Australia and New Zealand, you will have opportunity to see how our emerging definition of leadership of practice has been influenced from a number of sources. As an Early Years Professional, you are expected to have graduate level knowledge and understanding of the principles that underpin quality practice. The reflective tasks in this chapter will support the application of this knowledge to your own practice and in the way you lead the practice of others.

After reading this chapter you should be able to:
- understand some of the classic leadership theories;
- discuss how these have been applied to research studies on leadership in the Early Years;
- reflect on how these might shape our understanding of leadership of practice in the Early Years;
- apply some of the insights from theory and research to your own practice.

This chapter is wide-ranging and will help you to reflect on how you influence and lead the practice of others in relation to a number of the Standards for Early Years Professionals, particularly S1–6.

Introduction

The history of all cultures is punctuated with the names of great leaders and there have always been particular people whom others will follow (Doyle and Smith, 1999): Mahatma Gandhi, Joan of Arc, Winston Churchill, and American Indian Chief Sitting Bull are but a few for the list is endless. But we need to ask two questions: firstly, what makes them 'great' and secondly, is 'great' always 'good'? When we think of leaders like Adolf Hitler and others who have led with a dictatorial style, we recognise that not all leadership has beneficial outcomes. Are good leaders born or can they be 'made'/trained? Although you will encounter much theory in this chapter, you should try to keep the focus on your own leadership opportunities and in particular consider the particular context in which you work and your role as leader of practice.

Theories of leadership

Numerous books have been written which focus on the development of our theoretical understanding of leadership (Yukl, 1989; Clark and Clark, 1990; Bass and Stogdill, 1990). Most of these belong more appropriately to the world of finance, commerce, politics and business. However, it is worth considering briefly those that have emerged as *classic* theories or models of leadership (Doyle and Smith, 1999). As you consider these, it will be helpful to think back to your own experience of being led and to your current experiences of leading practice. Is there any particular model which 'speaks to' or resonates with your situation?

We have already identified that an absolute definition of leadership is hard to find. However, we have stated that in the context of EYPS, leadership is usually linked to the concept of the 'leader'. If we assume this, four key themes stand out:

1. to lead involves influencing the behaviour of others;

2. where there are leaders there are followers;

3. leaders seem to come to the fore when there is a crisis or special problem. In other words, they often become visible when an innovative response is needed;

4. our expectation is that leaders are people who have a clear idea of what they want to achieve and why.

Thus, good leaders are generally thought to be people who are able to think and act creatively in routine and non-routine situations and who set out to influence the actions, beliefs and feelings of others (Doyle and Smith, 1999).

Over the past few decades, there have been four main 'generations' of leadership theory:

- trait theories;

- behavioural theories;

- situational or contingency theories;

- transformational theories.

As van Maurik (2001) has pointed out, it is important to recognise that the four 'generations' are not mutually exclusive or totally time-bound but each has something to contribute to our overall understanding of leadership theory.

Trait theories

What is it that makes someone exceptional in this respect? The people in history who have been labelled great leaders have very different qualities. Bennis (1998) suggests that strong leaders know what they want, why they want it and how to communicate this to others in order to gain cooperation. Early trait research by Stogdill (1948), Mann (1959) and others suggested that there might be personality characteristics that appear to differentiate leaders from followers. Later work (such as Wright, 1996) refutes this and has found no differences between leaders and followers with respect to these characteristics and even found some evidence that people who possessed them were *less* likely to become leaders. Nevertheless, many of the popular books on the subject today still include a list of traits that are thought to be central to effective leadership. Gardner's (1989) study of North American organisations and leaders produced a list of traits or attributes for effective leadership that included physical vitality and stamina, intelligence and action-oriented judgement, task competence, the capacity to motivate people, trustworthiness and decisiveness.

A more recent study in the UK (Horne and Stedman Jones, 2001) identified the following key characteristics that leaders of organisations should possess: knowledge, inspiration, strategic thinking, a sense of vision and courage.

REFLECTIVE TASK

We need to be careful that we do not assume that all leadership is essential in groups and organisations as this relies on a deficit model of human beings, which implies that without a leader we are 'lost'. Do you think the trait theory of leadership tends to support this deficit model? Looking again at the traits described above (Gardner, 1989; Horne and Stedman Jones, 2001) do you believe any of these are important aspects of the EYP leadership role?

One of the issues often raised about trait theories concerns their apparent 'maleness' (Rosener, 1997; Rodd, 2006). When men and women are asked about each other's characteristics and leadership qualities, some significant patterns emerge. Both tend to have difficulties in seeing women as leaders. Indeed, the attributes on these lists are often viewed as male and this has particular relevance to Early Years practice with its predominantly female workforce. Rodd (2006) and Siraj-Blatchford and Manni (2007) discuss this notion in detail in relation to Early Years practice. This matter is addressed further in Chapter 4.

Behavioural theories

Many of the attributes listed by Gardner (1989) are, in fact, *behaviours*. This was a natural development of leadership theory: a move towards what leaders do, rather than the qualities they demonstrate. This became very much the way of understanding leadership during the 1960s. Different patterns of behaviour were grouped together and labelled as leadership 'styles'. The most notable product of the approach was Blake and Mouton's Managerial Grid, which was designed to diagnose and develop people's style of working. The four main styles of leadership that emerged are: *concern for task*, where the leader looks for high levels of productivity in order to achieve objectives; concern *for people*, where the needs of individuals are given high priority; *directive leadership*, where leaders take decisions for others; *and participative leadership*, where there is a shared decision-making process (Blake and Mouton, 1964, cited in Wright, 1996: 36–7)

Increasingly, limitations on this behavioural approach were identified (McGregor, 1970) and later studies (Sadler, 1997) suggested that it was difficult to state categorically that style of leadership was significant in determining whether it was successful or not. In fact, neither trait nor behavioural theories take sufficient account of the *context* in which leadership takes place. The style and behaviour of leaders are affected considerably by those they are working with and the environment in which they are working.

REFLECTIVE TASK

Consider the four types of leadership behaviours summarised by Wright (1996) above. Do any of these resonate with your experience of being 'led' in the past? Think particularly of Wright's concept of 'participative leadership' and how this links to the core skill of the EYP role in leading and supporting others.

Situational or contingency theories

Given the limitations of trait and behavioural theories of leadership, researchers began to focus on the *contexts* in which leadership is exercised, with the ensuing notion that there are a number of variables to be considered. Various views emerged, the most extreme being that just about everything was determined by the contexts, while style and behaviour counted for virtually nothing. However, most writers brought the idea of style with them, believing that particular contexts would demand particular forms of leadership. Thus, the key to effective leadership is seen to be the ability to work in different ways, to change the style to suit the situation. Can you see that this might have particular relevance for the EYP role as leader of practice?

Developing from situational theories of leadership, a *contingency* approach began to emerge. For instance, Fiedler and Garcia argued that effectiveness depends on two interacting factors: leadership style and the degree to which the situation gives the leader control and influence. They described three things as important here:

- the relationship between the leaders and followers: if leaders are liked and respected they are more likely to have the support of others;

- the structure of the task: if the task is clearly spelled out as to goals, methods and standards of performance then it is more likely that leaders will be able to exert influence;

- position power: if an organization or group confers powers on the leader for the purpose of getting the job done, then this may well increase the influence of the leader.
(Adapted from Fiedler and Garcia, 1987: 51–67)

This builds on Hersey and Blanchard's (1977) influential work on the importance of choosing the appropriate style for the particular situation. They identify four different leadership styles that can be used in different situations: *telling*, which concentrates on the task but is less concerned with relationships; *selling*, which concentrates on the task but is also very concerned with the relationship; *participating*, which concentrates on relationships but is less concerned with the task; and *delegating*, which does not concentrate on the task and is less concerned with relationships. Look back at your response to the Reflective task above. Which of Hersey and Blanchard's four leadership styles is most relevant to leadership of practice in the Early Years?

Leadership and the cultural context

Some writers have explored different patterns of leadership linked with men and women (Marshall, 1994). It is suggested that women may have leadership styles that are more nurturing, caring and sensitive, with a tendency to the *selling* model (Hersey and Blanchard, 1977). We revisit this theme in a later chapter but it is important to guard against over-generalising here. Any contrasts between the styles of men and women may be down to the situation and culture. In management, for example, women are more likely to be in positions of authority in people-oriented sectors such as personnel management, so this more nurturing style is likely to be emphasised. It should also be noted that most of the theorists/writers identified so far are from North America and the issue of cultural bias must be acknowledged. There is a great deal of evidence to suggest that cultural factors influence the way that people carry out, and respond to, different leadership styles. For example, some cultures are more individualistic, or value family as against bureaucratic models, or have very different expectations about how people address and talk to each other. Chakraborty's study (2003) suggests that leadership in the East is dominantly 'feminist-intuitive' whereas that in the West is 'masculine-rational'.

REFLECTIVE TASK

How important do you think the 'context' of leadership is? What contextual factors can you identify that facilitate your ability to lead practice effectively in your setting? Are there any hindering factors?

Transformational theories

Transforming leaders are visionary leaders who seek to appeal to their followers' 'better nature and move them toward higher and more universal needs and purposes' (Bolman and Deal, 1997: 314). In other words, the leader is seen as a change agent. It is this model that has particular relevance for you as you seek to demonstrate your EYP skills as a leader of change.

Earlier, Burns (1978) had drawn a distinction between 'transactional' (giving the followers one thing for another – a kind of 'trade-off') and 'transformational' leadership, though tended to set these as two polar opposites. However, Bass (1985) suggests that, rather than emphasising the differences between them, we should focus on how we might use elements of both types.

The transactional leader:

- recognizes what it is that we want to get from work and tries to ensure that we get it if our performance merits it;

- exchanges rewards and promises for our effort;

- is responsive to our immediate self-interests if they can be met by getting the work done.

The transformational leader:

- raises our level of awareness, and our level of consciousness about the significance and value of designated outcomes, and ways of reaching them;

- gets us to transcend our own self-interest for the sake of the team, organization or larger polity;

- alters our need level (after Maslow, 1986) and expands our range of wants and needs.

(Based on Bass, 1985; Wright, 1996)

REFLECTIVE TASK

Reflect on the difference between 'transactional' and 'transformational' models of leadership as shown here. Can you think of some examples from your own leadership practice where you have exercised transactional and/or transformational leadership?

Alongside the classic theories that underpin our comprehension of leadership, there are three main groups of writers who have helped inform and shape contemporary understanding. There are those who emphasise the team dimension of leadership and the role of team leader – such as Belbin (1993). Then there are those who describe the leader as a catalyst of change, such as Bennis (1998) and Covey (1989). Finally, there are those who see the leader as strategic visionary, such as Senge (1994). These three aspects of leadership are interconnecting and equally important.

While we remain in the broad arena of classic leadership theories, two further concepts are considered: those relating to *authority* and *charisma*. Authority within organisations is usually viewed as 'the possession of powers based on a formal role' (Heifetz, 1994:). This is how you might see your line manager. Do leaders have the same power? Doyle and Smith (1999) suggest that where leaders have the power to sack, demote or disadvantage, this may well result in compliance but not necessarily respect. They argue that the authority of the leader is rather more subtle and includes the ability to deal with crises and to manage change without being fazed by any challenges or obstacles. Leaders may have formal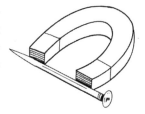

authority, but rely to a large extent on informal authority and influence, which flows from their personal qualities and actions and generates the respect of their peers.

Doyle and Smith (1999) describe formal authority as both a resource and a constraint. On the one hand it can bring access to systems and resources and, if handled well, it can help people feel safe. On the other hand, formal authority carries a set of expectations which are often quite unrealistic. The EYP is likely to have informal authority and influence and this can be an advantage in leading practice: This can be an advantage. The leader has greater freedom of movement and more choice to focus on specific issues (for the EYP 'practice') rather than having to maintain the organisation's focus (Doyle and Smith, 1999).

REFLECTIVE TASK

How does the concept of 'authority' and 'influence' sit with the emergence of EYPS? How is authority defined within the EYP role? In what ways do you believe you work with authority and in what ways do you influence others' practice?

The concept of the *charisma* of the leader has been central to our traditional understanding of leadership. The literal meaning of the word is 'a gift of grace, or of God' (Wright, 1996: 194) but its meaning in use is very difficult to articulate – although most people have a good inner sense of what constitutes a charismatic leader. When discussing charisma, we are in the arena of traits and qualities once more: the charismatic leader has particular skills, personality and presence. However, this is only one side of the notion of charisma and it is equally important to explore the situations or contexts in which charisma manifests itself. In times of distress – personally, within families, organisations and nationally – there is a tendency to seek figures who provide answers and demonstrate strength of purpose. Think of the role of Winston Churchill in the Second World War or Martin Luther King fighting against racial injustice in the southern states of the USA. In these examples, the emergence of the charismatic leader is interactional, that is it originates from a collective need for one to lead within a particular context.

The role of the charismatic leader, however, can also include heavy dependency. It can mean the loss of individual autonomy and relinquishing responsibility. Such leaders can be placed on an impossible pedestal and a huge gulf can grow between 'me' and 'him/her'. It can create a sense of invincibility and power in the leader and a corresponding sense of powerlessness in those who are led. It can also lead to significant conflict when the tide turns against the charismatic leader.

CASE STUDY

Adrienne is appointed as the new manager of a private day nursery. She arrives with extensive experience in Early Years in schools and has also worked in South America as an Early Years teacher in a charity project for street children. The nursery has just had a poor

Ofsted report but Adrienne approaches this as a challenging opportunity, not simply a concern. She is highly energetic, has huge self-confidence, is striking to look at with her jet-black long curly hair and has a very positive disposition. Very quickly, the whole nursery staff warms to her; the children love her, the parents engage well with her and she always has lots to share with staff in the weekly staff meetings. Moreover, Adrienne spends as much time as she can in the various base rooms, modelling new approaches to practice to the staff team. Very quickly, there are significant changes to many aspects of practice across the nursery.

REFLECTIVE TASK

- *In what ways has Adrienne used authority and charisma effectively here?*
- *In what ways does Adrienne exemplify effective leadership?*
- *What are the potential pitfalls?*

We have outlined the main theoretical frameworks that inform our understanding of leadership. Perhaps you have noticed that these insights sit fairly comfortably with the forms of organisation that are common in business, the armed forces, Government and so on. There have also been a number of research studies carried out relating to leadership in school settings (Harris et al., 2003; DfES and Price Waterhouse Coopers, 2007). Whilst these have had some influence on our understanding of leadership in the Early Years context, there remain distinctive differences to leadership in the Early Years – not least because of the diversity and scale of the sector. The emphasis of the roles and responsibilities identified for school leaders in the *National Standards for Headteachers* and reviewed in the 2007 study (DfES/Price Waterhouse Coopers: vii–viii) is on providing strategic direction and ethos, developing and managing people, networking and collaboration between schools and with other agencies, managing operations and delivery and accountability. Whilst this has some parallels with the role of leader/manager in an Early Years setting, these roles and responsibilities are very different from those identified in the EYP role. The roles and responsibilities of a children's centre leader/manager outlined in *National Standards for Leaders of Sure Start Children's Centres* (DfES/Sure Start, 2007) do have some similarities to those of the EYP, even identifying knowledge of the importance of observations of children as important.

REFLECTIVE TASK

Take a look at the National Standards for Leaders of Sure Start Children's Centres. Can you identify any other elements of these standards that apply to your understanding of the role of EYP?

In Chapter 1, we identified the lack of clear distinction in the literature so far between 'leader' and 'manager' in Early Years settings. What we are seeking to establish is a new paradigm of leadership – particularly one that sits with the EYP concept of 'leader of practice'. As we now move to consider some of the key writers and research studies in the field of leadership in early childhood, we should remind ourselves that these do not yet take full account of this emerging concept. What they do offer, however, are insights into issues that relate specifically to the complex field of leadership in Early Years settings in all their diversity.

Leadership in the Early Years

Smith and Langston's work (1999) is one of the key texts that must be acknowledged in any review of literature on leadership in the Early Years, though the focus of their work is very much that of managing staff. Nevertheless, their writing offers useful insights into the distinctions between leadership and management roles and warns of some of the inappropriate behaviours of the leader/manager that can result in ineffective teamwork. In particular, drawing on the earlier work of Shea (1993) and Bryman (1986), Smith and Langston offer a self-appraisal tool whereby leaders can identify current behaviours within their role and also reflect on what would be preferable behaviours.

PRACTICAL TASK

Especially linked to standards 1–6

Table 2.1 shows the leadership behaviours identified by Smith and Langston (1999: 11–12). Reflect on the way you demonstrate leadership in your setting and illustrate with an example from practice.

Table 2.1 Leadership behaviours

Leadership behaviour:	Example from practice:
Inspires	
Thinks	
Motivates	
Initiates change	
Dictates	
Takes decisions	
Sets objectives	
Sets the pace	
Inspires loyalty	
Self-sufficient	

The work of Jillian Rodd (1996, 1997, 1999) has made a significant contribution to the understanding of leadership in the Early Years and, indeed, is highly respected internationally. She writes from the perspective of over 30 years' experience and research in the early childhood field and has listened to and consulted widely with practitioners in all sectors, with parents, school staff, academic educators and policy makers. Clearly, Rodd's contribution to shaping and informing our understanding of the nature of leadership in the Early Years and its impact on professionalism in the field is hugely significant.

Rodd has contributed greatly to the bank of emerging research evidence relating to leadership in the Early Years but is also one of many to highlight the 'paucity of high quality research in this area' (Muijs et al., 2004: 166). Along with others (see for instance Sylva et al., 1999), she strongly believes the evidence of a clear link between effective leadership and organisational performance. In her early study, Rodd (1996) reported that insights from mainstream understanding of leadership were filtering into Early Years practice, although there was little understanding of roles like research, marketing or communication with policy makers as part of the leadership task, and no conception of risk-taking, change management or the creation of professional networks. In her 1997 study of 79 managers of Early Years settings, Rodd found that there was far more emphasis on *maintenance* (i.e. management) of an organisation than on *development* (i.e. leadership), though there was general consensus regarding the need for further (preferably in-service) training on the leadership aspects of the role.

From her research in both the UK and Australia, Rodd (1997) developed a 'typology of early childhood leadership' in which she argues that a key factor is that of length of experience in the leadership role. Rodd defined a set of generic personal characteristics, professional skills and roles and responsibilities which change/deepen over time from a leadership role of 'direct care' to one of 'indirect care'.

CASE STUDY

Marge, 44, has worked as an Early Years practitioner since she was 18. She has continued to progress academically (including achieving an early childhood studies degree) and her career has developed to the point that she has been the manager of a 68-place day nursery for the past seven years. Marge is outgoing and confident and competent in her role in maintaining the smooth running of the nursery. There is a low staff turnover and a healthy waiting list of children to attend.

Khalid, 35, has a fine arts degree and worked as an illustrator of children's books (which he still does freelance and part-time) for some years. When he was 30 he decided he wanted to work directly with children so completed a NVQ3 Early Years qualification whilst working in a private nursery setting. Last year, he became the joint leader of a voluntary pre-school in a suburban area and is already strongly influencing the children's opportunities for artistic expression in the setting.

What different approaches to leadership might Marge and Khalid bring to their respective roles? Do you think that 'length of service' is a factor here? What other factors might influence their leadership styles and roles?

At the end of the previous chapter, you considered the work of Janet Moyles, whose research (2006) led to the development of the Effective Leadership and Management Scheme for the Early Years (ELMS–EY). This was developed in response to the lack of training opportunities available to those who lead and manage Early Years settings. Moyles consulted widely with a range of leaders and managers in different Early Years settings to co-investigate the components of effective Early Years leadership and management. If you turn back to page 7, you will see that Moyles does identify the particular strand of 'leadership qualities' as one of the four 'branches' of the ELMS–EY model, alongside 'management skills', 'professional attributes' and 'personal characteristics and attitudes'. There are notable links here with the classic leadership theories and Moyles identifies *skills*, *qualities*, *attributes*, *characteristics* and *attitudes* as all necessary for the overall roles of leadership and management.

Can you begin to reflect on the particular skills, qualities, attributes, characteristics and attitudes which you already bring to the role of EYP? Are you also able to identify those where there are areas for development?

In Chapter 1, we considered some recent work by Siraj-Blatchford and Manni (2007) which builds on earlier studies, in particular *Researching Effective Pedagogy in the Early Years (REPEY)* (Siraj-Blatchford et al., 2002) and *Effective Provision of Pre-school Education (EPPE)* (Sylva et al., 2004). These two studies combine to create a representative picture of pre-school effectiveness and identify a clear correlation between 'strong leadership' (particularly where some of the staff are graduates or teacher-trained) and 'children's progress' (Siraj-Blatchford and Manni, 2007: 1). Children's progress is also linked to adults who have a good understanding of 'appropriate pedagogical content' and the pedagogue role. These studies have further strengthened our understanding and expectations of the EYP role.

The Effective Leadership in the Early Years (ELEYS) project (Siraj-Blatchford and Manni, 2007) was developed in response to the ongoing investment in the Children's Workforce. Since 1997, Government spending on childcare and pre-school education has already exceeded £1.7billion and the new Early Years provision that is emerging requires skilled leadership. Siraj-Blatchford and Manni (2007: 1) ask: 'Where is the firm evidence regarding the characteristics of effective leadership in Early Years settings?' It is this question which the ELEYS study seeks to address. Drawing on some of the insights from classical leadership theory, they conclude that the role of leadership in the Early Years is essentially that of 'leadership for learning' (Siraj-Blatchford and Manni, 2007: 12) where the fundamental requirements for the role are as follows:

- **contextual literacy** – situational leadership; consideration of the situation in which the leader operates and the people s/he is leading;

- **a commitment to collaboration** – where effective pedagogic and parental support are complementary and where there are effective inter-agency partnerships;

- **a commitment to the improvement of outcomes for all children** – where children's development is considered holistically and where individual needs are identified and met.

REFLECTIVE TASK

Can you link these elements of the leadership role identified by Siraj-Blatchford and Manni (2007) to the EYP Standards? Focus particularly, though not exclusively, on Standards 1–6.

Although Rodd, Moyles and Siraj-Blatchford are based mainly in the UK, they have all gained international respect and draw widely on insights and studies from other parts of the world. The review by Muijs et al. (2004) of the available literature on leadership in early childhood nevertheless offers a succinct summary of much of the research to date. Apart from noting the limited research available, they identify some key themes that need to be explored, and these are outlined below.

How important is leadership in the Early Years?

Confirming the findings of the EPPE project (Sylva et al.,2004) and Rodd's (1997) work and citing further studies (Stipek and Ogana, 2000; Bloom, 1997), Muijs et al. (2004) state the clear links between effective leadership and the quality of early childhood provision. Further, they draw on studies which show a link between effective leadership and low staff turnover which in turn relates to a higher quality learning environment (Hayden, 1997). Studies from the US 'Head Start' Programme show that competent and stable leadership is essential to the effectiveness of programme implementation (Ramey et al., 2000).

What are the main roles of leaders in the Early Years?

The overwhelming picture emerging from a review of the available research is that leaders in early childhood have a 'multiplicity of roles which are context specific' (Muijs et al., 2004: 161). A separate study by Hujala (2004) in Finland confirms that, within the Scandinavian context, early childhood leadership is determined to a large extent by factors specific to a particular setting, ranging from the way the early childhood leader sees his/her role within the team, to the way s/he is viewed within the community, to national legislation and policy on 'leadership'. Interesting data emerges from the New Zealand Educational Leadership Project (Hatherley and Lee, 2003) where 'leadership stories' offer insights into aspects of the role, including: having a strong vision; being able to articulate this in practice; strengthening links between the setting and the community; developing a community of learners; community advocacy; and giving children leadership opportunities. This aspect of 'community leadership' is also identified by Kagan and Hallmark (2001) while a study by Kunesh and Farley (1993) described an important leadership role as that of coordination between family, school and community. This is confirmed in later research by Atkinson et al. (2002), who review the impact of multi-agency working in, for instance, local Sure Start projects. A key factor in such work is effective leadership.

What are the characteristics of effective leaders in the Early Years?

Whilst identifying major weaknesses in the research base in this area, Muijs et al. (2004) draw on work by Bloom (2000) which concludes that early childhood leaders need to demonstrate competence in three areas which include those specifically relating to early childhood and to broader leadership:

- *knowledge* – including child development, pedagogical strategies, group dynamics and organisational theory;

- *skills* – including technical, human and conceptual skills (e.g. budgeting); and

- *attitudes* – including a sense of moral purpose.

How much professional development and training is there for leaders in the Early Years?

Here Muijs et al. (2004) find the lack of leadership development programmes to be a key issue in early childhood. They contrast the wide-ranging opportunities offered to leaders in school settings with the dearth of these for early childhood settings. In both the US (Bloom, 1997) and UK (Rodd, 1997) studies, leaders of early childhood settings reported that they had received no previous training on leadership and management skills before taking up their roles. A similar study in Australia (Hayden, 1997) found that 44 per cent of early childhood 'directors' had studied management subjects as part of their initial training. The general consensus in all these studies, however, was that training would be more meaningful once they were doing the job. A more promising picture is emerging, according to Muijs et al. (2004), who cite examples from the USA of the establishment of early childhood leadership programmes (Mitchell and Serranen, 2000). Although their review precedes the development of the NPQICL, Muijs et al. (2004) recommend that the framework offered by the National College of School Leadership be used as a model for similar developments in Early Years practice.

REFLECTIVE TASK

Why do you think there is a lack of high quality research on leadership in early childhood?

Since the review by Muijs et al. (2004) of the available literature, Whalley (2005b), who works as an advisor to the Minister and the Children and Families Directorate, has been leading on the development and 'roll-out' of the NPQICL programme. The methodology for this new pathway is itself based on effective leadership principles: a constructivist approach to teaching and learning; establishing links between leadership and learning; focus on task and process; focus on practitioner research; reflective journalling (keeping a reflective journal); and exploring the dynamic between theory and practice and between reflection and action. Although the model for the EYP as leader of practice is distinctively different from that offered through the NPQICL, such principles nonetheless are shared and you may want to reflect on how you apply them to your own role.

C H A P T E R   S U M M A R Y

In this chapter, we have once again acknowledged the influence of key writers in the field of leadership in the Early Years. We have reviewed much of the recent literature and you have had the opportunity to begin to apply some of the key insights from it to your own role as a leader of practice. There needs to be much more high-quality research on leadership in early childhood. From the research studies that do exist, there is clear evidence about the importance of the leadership role, the complexity of its function and the need for more specific training programmes and professional development. Since the publication of the review by Muijs et al. (2004) the National Professional Qualification for Integrated Children's Centre Leadership (NPQICL) has been established but, as noted, this is really aimed at creating a bank of professional leaders of integrated settings and is not a generic training programme for all early childhood leaders. At present, there are no existing empirical studies which relate to leadership of practice in the Early Years, although Siraj-Blatchford and Manni's ELEYS project (2007) comes close with its concept of 'leadership for learning'. Clearly, as you seek to identify opportunities in your own practice to demonstrate your competence as a leader of practice, you will be contributing to a wider canvas of understanding of this crucial role.

Moving on

As EYPs, one of your key roles is to lead others in creating an inclusive and anti-discriminatory ethos in your setting. In the next chapter, the focus moves towards the child/ren in the setting and their families and confirms the importance of the *context* of leadership. You will have further opportunity to think of the families represented in your setting and the community in which you work. If you have attended any relevant in-service training or professional development opportunities on equality practice, re-read your notes and reflect especially on your key role in cascading information to colleagues and leading change.

FURTHER READING

Muijs, D., Aubrey, C., Harris, A. and Briggs, M. (2004) How do they manage? A review of the research in early childhood. *Journal of Early Childhood Research*, 2: 157. Available at http://ecr.sagepub.com/cgi/content/abstreact/2/2/157.

Siraj-Blatchford, I. and Manni, L. (2007) *Effective Leadership in the Early Years Sector: The ELEYS Study*. London: The Institute of Education, University of London. Available at: http://www.gtce.org.uk/shared/contentlibs/126795/93128/120213/eleys_study.pdf.

3 Leadership of equality practice

CHAPTER OBJECTIVES

In this chapter, the focus moves to leadership of inclusive practice and the role of the leader in identifying and challenging anti-discriminatory practice. Definitions are explored and relevant legislation and statutory frameworks are outlined as we consider how the leader of practice should act as a role model in promoting appropriate values and principles – so central to the Early Years Foundation Stage framework. The role of the leader as one who 'creates a community', embracing diversity, is explored and, through case studies and other tasks, there are opportunities for reflection on the opportunities and challenges for leadership of practice.

After reading this chapter you should be able to:
- reflect on how you model and promote appropriate values and principles relating to equality;
- appraise critically how you identify and respond to the needs of each unique child;
- apply an appropriate understanding of how you can lead and support equality practice in your setting especially in dealing with discriminatory practices.

This chapter focuses particularly on Standards 2, 4, 12, 18, 23

Introduction

Good practice for equality is partly a focus on the individual children and families in your setting . . . But also covers the image of the world that you are giving children: the big picture that extends beyond their own back yard.

(Lindon, 2006:3)

In the previous chapter, we saw that there was much emphasis on the importance of the *situational* nature of leadership, particularly in the theories of Fiedler and Garcia (1987) and Moyles (2006). Siraj-Blatchford and Manni (2007: 12) refer to this as 'contextual literacy' and describe it as situational leadership where the leader is totally conversant with the particular context in which s/he operates and the people s/he is leading.

In carrying out your leadership role as an EYP, it is important that you engage whole-heartedly with the particular context in which you are working as a leader of practice. This includes knowledge and understanding about the children and their families, the staff in the setting and wider knowledge of the local community. In turn, the 'local' needs to be seen in the framework of the wider national and even international context.

In this chapter, we start by defining what we mean by 'equality practice' and reflect on where we have come from in our understanding of the concept, starting with a brief review of relevant legislation and critical issues in Early Years practice. We then focus on current challenges and opportunities and ask questions about how we can best take equality practice forward into the future. You will be encouraged to consider how you can best develop innovative ideas for the individual child and motivate and support others in their practice.

The legislative framework

One of the four key themes in the framework for the Early Years Foundation Stage (EYFS) (DCSF, 2008a) is that of 'the unique child' with a stated commitment that diversity of individuals and communities is valued and respected and no child or family is dis-criminated against.

Indeed, this chapter might have been more appropriately entitled 'leadership for the needs of the unique child' as we intend to identify many factors that need to be taken into account in building up a bank of knowledge and understanding about each individual as we work towards '"equalising" opportunities for those children and families whose situation or group identity may place them at a disadvantage' (Lindon, 2006: 3).

REFLECTIVE TASK

Think of recognisable attributes that help us identify each child's uniqueness: gender; ability; age/stage of development; ethnicity; culture; religion; language; socio-economic factors; in-child factors (personality, learning preferences etc).

- *Are there any other factors you think should be added here?*

- *How do you lead others to gather essential information about a new child coming into your setting?*

- *How is this information shared on a 'need to know' basis with other team members? What is your role as leader of practice in this?*

There are many complex issues relating to equality practice, most of which are beyond the parameters of the present discussion. At risk of over-simplification of these issues, a précis of the past fifty years or so in the UK shows that we have moved from a position of identifying disadvantaged or different families as a 'problem' to seeking to assimilate them into the 'mainstream' of society. From the 1980s onwards, legislative changes and increasing social awareness have led to a celebration of diversity. Initially legislation relating to equality focused on identifying discriminatory actions and making these unlawful. Gradually, there has been a shift in emphasis to placing an active duty on promoting equality. As EYPs, you have a professional responsibility to understand something of our social history, of the key changes in the law and how these have informed and shaped policy and practice in the Early Years.

REFLECTIVE TASK

Look at the following list relating to equality law and other legislation concerning the welfare of children. An internet search will enable you to find out more about any of these. What is the main impact on Early Years provision/practice of each of these pieces of legislation? How do these affect your role? Note down your answers:

- *Equal Pay Act (1970)*

- *Sexual Discrimination Act (1975)*

- *Race Relations Act (1976) with Amendment Act (2000)*

- *Disability Discrimination Act (1995)*

- *Special Educational Needs and Disability Act (2001)*

- *Equality Act 2006*

- *Children Acts 1989, 2004*

- *1989 United Nations Convention on the Rights of the Child – especially Articles 2, 14, 20 and 30. (Childcare Act, 2006)*

Dickins (2002) believes that equality of opportunity has always been given prominence in Early Years practice but the direction of travel of policy and legislation over the past two decades has encouraged and consolidated this. Particularly influential here have been the Children Act 1989, the Rumbold Report (DES, 1990), *Curriculum Guidance for the Foundation Stage* (QCA 2000), the *Birth to Three Matters* framework (DfES, 2002) and the National Standards set to regulate childcare provision (DfES, 2001). Commitment to meeting the needs of all children and improving outcomes for them is central to the Early Years Foundation Stage framework (DCSF, 2008a) and enshrined in the Childcare Act 2006. EYP Standards 2, 4, 12, 18, 23 remind you that this is a critical part of your role as leader of practice.

The words and language we use are of enormous importance in any consideration of equality practice. First of all there is the need for precision of language, as there are a number of terms relating to equality practice and definitions are not always firmly agreed. Secondly, the EYP has a responsibility to observe reactions to spoken and non-verbal language and, where necessary, adjust these in the light of these reactions even if there is no deliberate intention of excluding any individual or being impolite. Lindon (2006) offers a very useful list of definitions and these are used here for clarity:

- **Equality Practice:** a move towards the common ground for different group identities, treating each with equal concern and responding specifically to any needs identified.

- **Promoting Equality/Equal Opportunities:** actions integral to regular practice in order to ensure that all children are enabled to have positive experiences supporting personal identity.

- **Anti-Discriminatory Practice:** an active attempt (where practitioners take the initiative) to promote positive attitudes and behaviour, to challenge and change negative outlooks and actions on the basis of any group identity.

- **Anti-Bias Practice or Curriculum:** a framework of activities, play materials and experiences that avoid unnecessary stereotypes and actively promote understanding and knowledge of all groups within society.

- **Inclusion:** this term, along with an **inclusive approach** was initially developed with reference to disability. These terms, and also the concept of **social inclusion**, are now generally applied to practice about equality. In essence, it means an active effort to address ways in which children or adults may be excluded – intentionally or unintentionally – from services or experiences. (Adapted from Lindon, 2006: 13)

REFLECTIVE TASK

Read and re-read Lindon's definitions above and think how these relate to Standards 2, 4, 12, 18, 23 in particular. From your own role, identify three examples of proactive practice work related to equality practice you have undertaken and show how you have supported others in equality practice.

Early Years Foundation Stage

The Statutory Framework for the EYFS (DCSF, 2008a) sets out the responsibilities of providers for equality practice very clearly.

Providers have a responsibility to ensure positive attitudes to diversity and difference – not only so that every child is included and not disadvantaged, but also so that they can learn from the earliest age to value diversity in others and grow up making a positive contribution to society. Practitioners should focus on each child's individual learning, development and care needs by:

- *Removing or helping to overcome barriers for children where these already exist;*

- *Being alert to the early signs of needs that could lead to later difficulties and responding quickly and appropriately, involving other agencies as necessary;*

- *Stretching and challenging all children.*

(DCSF, 2008a: 1.14)

All registered settings for children from birth to five are now required to demonstrate compliance to this statutory framework and most do this through written policy statements which may be called 'Equality of Opportunity', 'Special Educational Needs (SEN) ' or 'Inclusion' policies, or a combination of these. All settings are required to have a designated member of staff in the role of Special Educational Needs Coordinator (SENCO) and some settings also have a designated Equality or Inclusion Coordinator. These policies need revision and rethinking on a regular basis.

Policy in action

Law, policy and rhetoric are all very well. The challenge for us all lies in translating the above into everyday good, reflective practice which demonstrates total commitment to the underpinning ethos and meaning of them.

> *Effective policy making is an active and dynamic process that ideally involves all the stakeholder groups including parents and children at some level.*
>
> (Dickins, 2002: 19)

Prescriptive or ready-made policies have their place but the most effective policies are ones where there is shared ownership and understanding of the contents. Only then can they be applied effectively. Dickins (2002) suggests that policy-making is an active and dynamic process which should involve all stakeholders, including parents and children, at some level. Skills in developing policies should be viewed as fundamental to the role of the EYP. A policy is a statement of intentions for your setting and should draw on the key principles and values that inform and guide your work and then identify a strategy of how these are put into practice. Your role as leader of practice may well include writing policy documents. Think about the following sections:

- key intentions, values or principles that guide practice;
- the general environment – accessibility, relevance, stimulation, safety etc.;
- the curriculum and programme of activities;
- parent/family involvement;
- staff training, development and support;
- roles and responsibilities of key individuals – such as key persons, SENCO, Inclusion Coordinator etc;
- monitoring policy implementation;
- timetables for implementation;
- publicity and dissemination policy;
- timetable for evaluation and review of policy.

(Based on Dickins, 2002; Lindon, 2006)

Almost certainly you will have at least one written policy statement relating to equality practice in your setting. Use the following questions to appraise the effectiveness of this at the present time.

PRACTICAL TASK

1. What current examples of equality practice involving children and families from your setting can you use to demonstrate that your policy/policies is/are working in an active way?

2. Are the details of the policy/policies clear to you and everyone in the team? What evidence do you have to support this?

3. Are the details of the policy/policies clear to the families in your setting? What measures do you have in place to ensure policies are accessible to all families? Do systems exist to regularly review how policy information is shared with all families?

4. How confident are you to share your practice with other professionals and if necessary, how would you/could you challenge advice that may conflict with your own principles for good practice?

5. How have you personally accessed and used opportunities for recent professional development in this area?

6. What are your information systems for ensuring that you are up to date with any changes in local or national guidance or how the law could affect your practice and setting?

7. In what ways have you led and supported others in your setting in equality practice?

(Based on Lindon, 2006)

Personal value stance

One of the most important ways you will demonstrate leadership of equality practice is through your personal value stance. If you are able to lead by example with a genuinely positive attitude to equality practice and a willingness to learn more and to reflect regularly on your understanding, this will make a vital difference to the ethos of your setting. Again, this is a complex area but as a reflective EYP, you need to be aware of your own personal and professional journey and particularly of the way you may have internalised stereotypes which affect the way you view and, consequently, have particular expectations of children and families. Such internalised layers operate on both a conscious and subconscious level. Acknowledging the extent to which our personal belief and value system influences what we bring to the Early Years environment is an important 'first step' en route to anti-discriminatory practice.

Consider some of the 'building blocks of your own identity' (Dickins, 2002) – such as gender ethnicity, class, religion and education.

Reflect on the significance of these in shaping who you are and what you believe.

* *Describe yourself in a sentence using these five attributes.*

- *In the EYP role as leader of practice, how do you ensure colleagues are aware of these influences on them and their roles?*

- *How, as a leader, do you give staff the skills and confidence to challenge appropriately overt inequality/ discriminatory practice they may witness?*

The Alliance for Inclusive Education (1990) offers nine core principles as indicative of commitment to inclusive practice. Use these as a further tool for reflection as you clarify your own personal values and beliefs:

- a person's worth is independent of their abilities or achievements;

- every human being is able to feel and think;

- every human being has a right to communicate and be heard;

- all human beings need each other;

- real education can only happen in the context of real relationships;

- all people need support and friendship from people of their own age;

- progress for all learners is achieved by building on things people can do rather than what they can't ;

- diversity brings strength to all living systems;

- collaboration is more important than competition.

Before we move on to think about particular strategies that support inclusive practice, it is important to conclude this section by focusing on the values that children themselves are developing. Again, this is a complex matter and expansive discussion is beyond the scope of this publication but it is important to reflect here on S28 and think about how the values and attitudes demonstrated by the EYP can directly affect and influence children's own values. The EYFS framework reminds us that:

> *The attitudes of young children towards diversity are affected by the behaviour of adults around them and by whether all children and families using the setting are valued and welcomed.*

> (DCSF, 2008c: 1)

Rodd (2006) reminds us that many of the subjective and enduring attitudes we use to interpret messages we receive from others are formed by the age of five. From our understanding of child development, we know that young children from around the age of two are visually curious about the people and places around them. They take note of physical characteristics: height, weight, skin colour, hair style, clothing, etc; of gender; and of some characteristics of disability – hearing aids, glasses, walking sticks etc. But we do know that whilst such very young children speak without any socially constructed

---

REFLECTIVE TASK

> *Young children's antennae readily tune in to both overt and subtle messages about who is 'better' than who and who is valued in society . . . and all this at a time when they are beginning to put together a picture of their own identity.*
>
> *(Dickins, 2002: 17)*

What are the implications of this for the EYP in modelling and leading equality practice? How do you support your colleagues to recognise, monitor and challenge, if inappropriate, subtle messages are being conveyed within the setting?

---

inhibitions, any questions or comments they make at this stage are **not** value-laden but merely an extension of their natural curiosity as they construct knowledge and understanding of their world. From the age of three years, some of their comments may appear to be value laden but these are almost always 'recycled adult comments' (Lindon, 2006:47). Devising and implementing appropriate ways to challenge such comments when necessary is an important aspect of the EYP role. However, it is important to register your valuable role in modelling to children the application of fair approaches and how you treat everyone with equal concern; this includes children, staff, parents, other professionals and any visitors.

The key person

The appointment of the 'key person' and the organisation of this is addressed more fully in Chapter 5 but we note here how integral to good equality practice the key person role is in 'meeting the needs of each child . . . and responding sensitively to their feelings, ideas and behaviour, talking to parents to make sure that the child is being cared for appropriately for each family' (DCSF, 2008a: 37).You will need to make sure that you understand the underpinning principles driving the new legislation and, within your role as EYP, seek to empower those in your setting in their roles as key persons. In larger settings, especially where staff work different shifts, it is best practice to designate a 'significant other' for each child to support the primary key person.

Whilst the crucial roles of key person and significant other cannot be overemphasised, it is important to create appropriate means for sharing vital information with all relevant staff about each child – especially linked to their individual learning journeys and stories (Carr, 2001) and how these connect into wider organisational matters such as planning and monitoring the programme and partnership with families.

CASE STUDY

In a busy base room for 18 two- to three-year olds, Liam is the key person for two-year-old Shafiq. But, as Shafiq attends the day nursery full-time from 8am until 6pm, Chloe has been appointed as co-key person for Shafiq. In this way, the nursery ensures that for most of the time that Shafiq is in nursery, either Liam or Chloe – or both of them – are also present and take lead responsibility for his well-being. Shafiq has been diagnosed with a hearing impairment (HI) and so once a week, a teacher from the local authority HI Education Service visits to work with Shafiq and to discuss his progress with one/both key workers and Shafiq's parents.

REFLECTIVE TASK

What are the challenges to the EYP in ensuring that all relevant personnel are involved, can contribute to the weekly meetings and work in partnership together? What opportunities does this present for the EYP to demonstrate equality practice?

The significance of the early years of a child's life in shaping personal identity has long been identified. Particularly crucial factors in developing a sense of self come from the following: knowing our own name – and how people use and react to it; an understanding of what it means to be a 'boy' or a 'girl'; our place within our immediate family – parents, siblings and other close relatives; how we look and how people react to our looks; what we can do and cannot do – and the extent to which this matters to people; a growing sense of 'what we do in our family/community'; experiences of cultural traditions, mother/father roles, religious faith and other significant beliefs/values within their daily life (based on Lindon, 2006).

It is important to take a holistic view of identity and the individual child and understand that the formation of identity is a complex and dynamic process which, though central to childhood, may be modified throughout adult life (Dickins, 2002).

REFLECTIVE TASK

A young child experiences the important people in her/his life as:

> *'helping me manage through the day, thinking about me, knowing me well, sometimes worrying about me, getting to know each other so they can all do the "best" for me and talking together about me and to me'*
>
> *(based on Roberts, 2006) .*

- *How have you developed key person practice to ensure it reflects your ethos/policy for equality and/or inclusion?*

REFLECTIVE TASK CONTINUED

- *How do you support children, families and practitioners when unfamiliar cultural or linguistic differences are part of the experiences the child brings to the setting?*

- *What are the challenges you have faced/may face and how might you plan to meet these in future?*

Staff development opportunities

EYP S38 reminds you of the importance of identifying and accessing relevant professional development for yourself and of supporting others in their continuing professional development (we discuss this further in the final chapter of the book). There are many workshops and training programmes available both within local authority provision and nationally. The CD-ROM provided as part of the resource to support implementation of the EYFS framework (DCSF, 2008c) signposts a range of these to support EYFS practice in meeting the needs of the unique child and promoting equality practice. Do make sure you access this superb resource to the full.

Current inequalities

Despite the priority and financial investment given over the past decade, in particular, to quality provision in the Early Years, to early intervention and to raising the status and professionalism within Early Years practice, there remain undoubted inequalities (see, for instance, Antoniou, 2005; Sure Start Keighley, 2005; Hirsch, 2007) and these should be of concern to all reflective EYPs. A report from the United Nations Children's Fund (UNICEF, 2007) makes for sobering reading. The UK scored a very low ranking from a study of 21 comparably industrialised countries in terms of children's well-being by the time they reach the age of 15.

In particular, we know that families from minority ethnic groups are not always accessing the Early Years provision and services to which they are entitled (Sure Start Keighley, 2005; Antoniou, 2005) and this is often because the diverse cultural and linguistic requirements of such families are not always taken fully into account by providers. Remember what we learned in Chapter 3 about the situational–contextual aspects of leadership? Further, families of children with special educational needs are not always able to access Early Years services and many of the recent evaluations of Sure Start projects (such as Sure Start Keighley, 2005) highlight the need for provision to be more inclusive, with further emphasis on identifying families affected by additional needs and closer liaison with health professionals in this. A report from the Pre-school Learning Alliance (Antoniou, 2005) paints a similar picture relating to children with special educational needs within voluntary pre-schools, highlighting some regional inequalities.

Edgington (2004) offers a useful checklist for awareness-raising in matters relating to equality practice. She asks you to consider how you have made yourself and your staff aware of the following: inequalities in society, inequalities in education, attitudes (including your own) which may lead to discrimination against some children and families, discriminatory language used or unthinking remarks made by staff, children, parents, visitors and practices within your own setting which may reinforce existing inequalities – especially admissions, transitions, communication with parents, and access to wider services (adapted from Edgington, 2004: 86).

CASE STUDY

Val *works as an EYP in a consultancy capacity across a small chain of private nurseries. The majority of these cater for the needs of white British children and families and the nursery environments and programmes reflect this. However, the neighbourhood of two of them is much more multicultural.*

How might Val lead practice to be more inclusive? In particular, what professional development opportunities might Val access for herself and/or develop for the nursery staff team?

CASE STUDY

Juan and Penny *co-lead a local pre-school in the local village hall. Historically, the setting has not catered for children with additional needs as such families had not registered for places. However, recently two families have requested places for their children: one has a significant medical condition and the other has mobility challenges.*

How might Juan and Penny best prepare themselves as leaders to create an inclusive setting for such children? What action will they need to take in leading the staff to feel ready and skilled to manage inclusion on a daily basis?

How do we take best equality practice forward?

Discrimination – whether direct, indirect, intentional or unintentional – comes in many forms and sound reflective practice will include vigilance to any/all of these. Standard 18 offers a reminder that it is the task of the EYP to support and lead the creation of an inclusive community and S39 focuses on the role of the EYP in 'taking a constructively creative and critical approach towards innovation' (CWDC, 2007a: 9). The setting stories and reflective tasks that follow offer you an opportunity to consider innovative ways of moving equality practice forward in your own setting and in so doing demonstrate more effective anti-discriminatory practice. Guidance from the EYFS framework offers helpful pointers for practitioners in meeting children's diverse needs and helping all children to make the best possible progress. It states that practitioners should:

- Extend the scope of individualised learning by providing challenging expectations and relevant, developmentally appropriate learning opportunities for babies and young children

- Provide a safe and supportive learning environment, free from harassment, in which the contribution of all children and their families is valued and where racial, religious, disability and gender stereotypes and all expressions of discrimination or prejudice are challenged

- Value the fact that families are all different – that children may live with one or both parents, with other relatives or carers, with same sex parents or in an extended family

- Work with parents to identify learning needs and respond quickly to any area of particular difficulty

- Plan appropriate opportunities that build on and extend all children's knowledge, experiences, interests and skills and develop their self-esteem and confidence in their ability to learn

- Use a wide range of teaching strategies, based on children's learning needs

- Provide a wide range of opportunities to motivate, support and develop children and help them to be involved, concentrate and learn effectively

- Plan for each child's individual care and learning requirements, including the additional or different provision required to meet particular individual needs

- Audit how accessible the setting is for children who use wheelchairs or other mobility aids or who are learning English as an additional language and take action to include a wider range of children

- Work together with professionals from other agencies to provide the best learning opportunities for each individual child.

(DCSF, 2008c: 2–3)

REFLECTIVE TASK

Be realistic in your appraisal of how far the reality of your own practice and setting is from these 'ideals'. Where might you start in the development of more effective and innovative practice in your setting?

You are now encouraged to use this series of setting stories. These are not exhaustive but are intended to be a reflective tool as you consider the potential breadth of equality practice and focus on its application to your own role and setting, especially as you think about gathering evidence for S2, 4, 12, 18, 23 and reflect on the ways you challenge discrimination. Some of the case studies here may well describe experiences you have not encountered so far in your role but it is important that you engage with these, particularly reflecting on the value stance and attitudes of staff, children and families portrayed in them, as well as on possible action. The responses made by staff in these scenarios are not necessarily the 'right' ones but they do indicate the three EYP core skills – the ability to:

- make decisions on the basis of sound judgement;

- lead and support others;

- relate to and communicate with others

(CWDC, 2007c).

Best practice in respect for girls and boys

Scenario 1: Cassie works as a registered childminder and is currently minding three children: a baby girl, Sophie, of nine months and two toddlers: Sophie's brother Damien, aged 26 months and Adela (different family), aged 27 months. Cassie is a committed and conscientious reflective practitioner who is increasingly working on the personalised approach to her provision ('possible lines of direction' – PLOD approach; Bruce et al., 1997) by observing and building on the children's interests. Adela and Damien enjoy dressing up and both love the character 'Bob the Builder' from the popular TV series. Cassie has provided hard hats, fluorescent sleeveless jackets and other artefacts to support the children in their fantasy play which takes place mainly in the garden. However, Adela's mum, Mandy, talks to Cassie about Adela dressing up in 'boys' clothes' and the rough-and-tumble nature of her play. Mandy asks that Adela wears only 'girls' clothes' when she dresses up.

Cassie listens attentively to Mandy's concerns – aware, nonetheless, of her own personal strong disagreement with Mandy's stance. Cassie responds with an expression of positive regard for Mandy and encourages her to express the core of her concern. Adela is the youngest of four children, with three older brothers, and Mandy is very keen that Adela should be 'feminine' in every way. Over some weeks, Cassie works with Adela and Mandy to reassure Mandy that gender roles are not fixed or determined by role or fantasy play and that any attempts to stop Adela playing in her own way with her friend, Damien, would be virtually impossible and not helpful to her development. Cassie also introduced a wider range of dressing up clothes and fantasy play over time. For instance, she helped the children create a 'cave' using her dining room table covered in dark cloth, which could be lifted to make an entrance. She provided torches and boxes so they could develop the play.

REFLECTIVE TASK

> Boys' under-achievement in education has now become a global concern . . .The Early Years represent a significant opportunity for this to be addressed.
>
> > (Connolly, 2004: foreword)

In what ways do you ensure that the needs of girls and boys are identified and met in your setting? How do you help lead everyone involved with the setting to understand an ethos that avoids stereotypes and challenges discrimination?

Best practice in respect of personal care

Scenario 2: Little Nook Pre-School is based in a semi-rural area and is generally white British, comfortably 'middle class', with high socio-economic stability. The leaders and staff team have built up a strong reputation and the setting is popular with local families.

A new family moved into the locality and their three-year-old daughter, Bayo, is registered to start at the pre-school. The family is Nigerian in origin and Bayo wears her hair in beautiful intricate braids. The staff team prepared well for Bayo's arrival in advance and

Tessa, the leader, and Sally, Bayo's assigned key person, carried out a home visit to build up a close profile of Bayo and her family before she started at the pre-school. They continued to work with her parents on supporting Bayo's transition into the setting. As it was not a customary 'starting' time for a child in the pre-school, prior to Bayo's first session, the children were informed about her impending arrival and staff led them in discussion about how best they might welcome her. At this stage, staff made no reference to Bayo's cultural heritage. The children suggested making a picture to welcome her and so staff developed the children's ideas of each one drawing or painting 'self-portraits' to create a huge 'Welcome to Bayo from Everyone in Little Nook Pre-School'. Bayo's mum, Sade, had told Tessa and Sally that Bayo's favourite storybook at the time was *I Want My Tent: Little Princess Story Book* (2007) by Tony Ross but that she also liked the story of *Handa's Surprise* by Eileen Browne (1995). Tessa selected this story for purchase and used it with the children two or three times before Bayo arrived. Again, before Bayo's first day, resources were supplemented to reflect more of Bayo's cultural heritage: additional books were shared by all the children, and the life play area was enhanced by lengths of brightly patterned material for dressing up and an authentic black doll.

Bayo's first couple days went very well and by day 3 her mum, Sade, was leaving her for up to two hours. Then, Sally and other staff noticed that some of the other children, particularly the girls in the pre-school, were fascinated by Bayo's hair, often touched it and began to ask her and the staff questions about it. Bayo appeared to be irritated or embarrassed by this and usually moved away when children touched her. The staff monitored this closely and normally used distraction strategies though these were only effective in the short-term.

At the end of the first week, Sally, with Tessa present, asked to speak to Sade, to ask her how she felt Bayo had settled. Sade reported that Bayo did not say much about pre-school but was quite happy at home. Sally shared the situation about Bayo's hair and together the three of them discussed the appropriate action. Sade offered to come in and show the children how she braided Bayo's hair and to braid some of the other children's hair on request. Tessa and Sally also worked with Sade to set up a 'hair dressing' area in the pre-school using resources from both cultures, including empty pots of hair products for both males and females and adding some rag dolls with long woollen hair for the children to practise braiding skills.

REFLECTIVE TASK

What strategies would you implement to ensure your setting's practice was inclusive and met the specific needs of the following children?

- *A girl with sensitive or troublesome skin;*

- *a boy, who is over three, who needs help with the toilet;*

- *those who have their hair covered or wear particular types of clothes – such as children from Sikh or Exclusive Brethren families.*

Best practice for different kinds of families

Scenario 3: Sunny Days Nursery offers provision for over 50 children aged from three months to five years. In the pre-school room, for three- to five-year-olds, there is a team of four staff working with 18 children, led by Gill who is a level-5 (with a Sector Endorsed Foundation Degree Early Years) qualified practitioner. Gill is a committed and conscientious reflective practitioner who seeks to lead by example in all areas of practice and provision in the toddler room.

Recently a family has moved into the neighbourhood and their four-year-old boy, Rory, has joined the group. When Gill (who is Rory's key person) – along with the nursery manager – carries out the home visit prior to Rory starting at the nursery, she learns that his mum, Sheena, lives with a female partner, Bernadette. This information is shared naturally as Gill builds up a log about Rory ('All About Me') and asks about all the 'important others' in Rory's life. Gill clarifies what names Rory uses for Sheena ('Mum') and Bernadette ('Bernie') and whether he has any contact with his biological father (he doesn't).

This is the first time that some of the staff in the room have experienced a child with same-sex parents and one of them, Rosie, makes hostile and insulting comments to Gill about such families. Gill uses the opportunity to raise Rosie's awareness of her own personal value stance (to which she is entitled, although the hope is that she can learn to be less discriminating), but reminds her that such attitudes are easily transmitted to children and may affect the way Rosie relates to Rory. Gill makes sure that new books in the nursery reflect a range of different types of families: traveller families; families with children with additional needs; families where mum goes to work and dad stays at home, as well as families with same-sex parents, those with two mums/dads, parents who live separately etc.

REFLECTIVE TASK

Reflect on how Gill tackled this situation. Would you have done anything differently in your setting? Does your setting cater for the needs of the diverse range of family structures that you might encounter?

Best practice for religious beliefs

Scenario 4: Sameena will shortly be returning to work as an accountant after the birth of her daughter, Sufia, who is 14 months old, and has registered her at Hey Diddle Diddle private nursery, near to her place of work. Tim is one of the staff in the under-twos room and he is assigned to be Sufia's key person. Tim, with the nursery manager, Kath, goes to visit Sameena and Sufia prior to Sufia starting at Hey Diddle Diddle. Sameena and her family, as Muslims, have strong views that only women should take responsibility for a baby's care needs and Sameena shares this politely during the home visit.

Kath and Tim respond sensitively but explain the way the key person system is organised in the nursery and that all practitioners share the same role. They both express respect for the religious beliefs of Sameena and her family but take a clear stance that if the issue of female care is not negotiable for Sameena, then Hey Diddle Diddle is not able to meet the family's needs. Kath goes on to outline the alternative of childminding provision as a way that Sameena can guarantee that Sufia has exclusively female care.

REFLECTIVE TASK

This is a difficult area as there are many strongly held views affecting childcare practice by the different religious groupings in contemporary society. How well informed do you consider yourself to be about these? How might you have dealt with the situation above? In what way was Kath demonstrating skills as a leader of practice here?

Best practice in respect of food and mealtimes

Scenario 5: Staff in an urban children's centre are generally well prepared when it comes to accommodating a range of dietary needs which allow for the different cultural and religious groups in the area and also for those children with medical needs. Three new children, Meg, Jack and Adem, from traveller families, are placed in the 'Tigers' room for three- and four-year-olds, with liaison/support from the local authority Traveller Education Service (TRES). The children have not been away from their families before. In consultation with TRES and the children's families, Meg, Jack and Adem are each assigned a separate key person in order to best monitor their needs at this key time of transition.

Whilst the children are slow to relate socially to the other children, they do gravitate towards each other during play and early observations are that they are using play purposefully and developmentally appropriately. It is the practice in the setting to use lunchtimes as social occasions with each key person sitting with his/her own key group. By week three, Meg, Jack and Adem are still showing signs of restlessness and anxiety at lunchtime and staff notice that they are eating very little.

The relevant staff members meet with the TRES liaison worker and the children's parents, and together they devise a strategy. Lunchtimes are developed to allow all of the children to play outside in small groups and Meg, Jack and Adem are then chosen to eat at the end of the lunchtime with the centre teacher at their table. He uses a 'social story' approach with the children at lunch, allowing them to serve themselves from the various foods on offer. Once the children are more confident in eating, a staged approach to their inclusion in the usual lunchtime arrangements will then be negotiated.

REFLECTIVE TASK

What terminology/language do you use when applying equity practice to food and meal times? Would you use phrases like 'restricted' or 'limited' diet? What do such phrases imply? Your own value stance is important here, especially in the way you lead practice. How do you cater for the needs of children with allergies or medical conditions affecting their diet? Is there any difference to your practice if/when dietary needs are determined by religious beliefs?

Best practice in respect of disability and ill health

Scenario 6: Guy and Estelle's third baby, Jonni, now aged ten months, is born with a medical condition that requires him to be fed by tube and have regular physiotherapy to ease congestion on his lungs. Their two older children were minded by Carol, a registered childminder, before they went to school and Estelle wishes to return to work part-time though is anxious about the additional needs that Jonni has. Carol and Estelle meet two months before Estelle is due to start back at work and days/hours are negotiated when Jonni will be Carol's sole charge. For the month before Estelle starts at work, she and Carol spend half a day a week together to jointly mind Jonni so that Estelle can supervise Carol in feeding procedures. The local Portage worker joins them for one of these sessions too, and the three of them agree on a shared approach to Jonni's individual development plan.

REFLECTIVE TASK

What experience have you had in leading the policy and practice of your setting in meeting the additional needs of children related to a medical condition, or who have a Statement of SEN? Consider how you have supported colleagues to work in partnership with other agencies and the challenges and developments this has created.

Best practice for more able children

Scenario 7: In Tree Tops Pre-School, Archie, aged three-and-a-half, is able to read fairly fluently, recognises numbers to 100 and can do simple mental calculations involving addition and subtraction. His parents are anxious not to 'hothouse' Archie, whose progress is otherwise typical of his age. The group leader, Sam, is Archie's key person but seeks to develop a whole team approach to the inclusion of Archie within the group. One of the team, Sandra, has a tendency to want to provide more formal opportunities (what Sandra believes to be 'school-type') in which Archie reads and performs mathematical operations and she brings in 'workbooks' that her own (older) children have used. She is observed 'testing' Archie by asking him to read to her and answer mental maths questions. Sandra refers to him as 'Little Einstein'.

Sam arranges a one-to-one meeting with Sandra to discuss the situation. She aims to get Sandra to understand the impact of her approach not only on Archie but on the other children. Her reaction is accentuating 'difference' between him and the rest in an unhelpful way. Of particular concern is the unconscious value stance that Sandra is demonstrating: that play is not the best medium for Archie's learning. Sam strongly believes that it is and that Archie needs to learn socially and collaboratively with others, whilst being offered appropriate developmental challenges through play-based activities suitable to his learning ability. This is not an easy time for Sam and Sandra's professional relationship but slowly they are able to work together more constructively for Archie's sake.

REFLECTIVE TASK

What experience have you had to date of supporting young children of exceptional ability? Sometimes these children have additional needs, such as some diagnosed on the autistic spectrum. In what ways has Sam exercised effective leadership of practice here? How does this link to S1?

Best practice in respect of different forms of communication

Scenario 8: Jean-Paul is two-and-a-half and has been in the UK for six months. His parents, Emilie and Raoul, came into the country as asylum seekers from a French-speaking country in Africa and the family now has refugee status. Emilie and Raoul are learning English but at home they speak mainly French to Jean-Paul who is not using much spoken language at all at the moment. Emilie has joined a local parent and toddler group so that she and Jean-Paul can develop friendships with other local families. Shazia, the coordinator of the parent and toddler group, is herself bilingual, with English as her second language, but does not speak French. One of the other parents, Kenny, is fairly fluent in French.

Emilie is committed to Jean-Paul being bilingual and Shazia herself knows the importance of 'children needing the contact with child speakers of any language because children use language in a different way from adults' (Lindon, 2006: 133). Together, Shazia, Emilie and Kenny work on a strategy which includes some use of French but mainly using English in the setting, and soon Jean-Paul is happy to leave Emilie's side and explore the range of play activities on offer with the other children.

REFLECTIVE TASK

Look at this guidance from the EYFS framework.

> *Practitioners should value linguistic diversity . . . provide opportunities for children to use their home language in play and learning . . . actively promote bi-lingualism as a strength . . . and encourage all children to learn some of the languages they hear around them . . . They should model this themselves by . . . greeting children and families in their home language.*
>
> *(DCSF, 2008c: 4)*

This guidance clearly reminds Early Years practitioners of the importance of a child's home language. How do you yourself model effective practice in building on the child's experience of language at home? How is this balanced with planning appropriate opportunities for all children to develop English? What are the challenges for the leader of practice here?

C H A P T E R   S U M M A R Y

This may have been a challenging chapter but you should see that the principles outlined in it provide sure and firm foundations for the leadership of equality practice which is fundamental to the EYP role. In the process of reviewing some of the key issues relating to equality and inclusive policy and practice, and the weight of law behind these, you have also been encouraged to grow in self-awareness about your own personal beliefs and value stance and to reflect on how these influence and impact on the children, families and staff in your setting as part of your leadership role. Throughout the case studies and reflective tasks there has been an implicit motif: that of challenging discriminatory practice in all its forms by modelling a positive approach to diversity.

Moving on

Having defined the new concept of leadership of practice, explored the existing literature and research studies on leadership in the Early Years and established the core element of equality practice for the role of EYP, we now turn to consider some of the essential qualities, skills and competencies required for the role. In some ways, this will build on the understanding of classic trait theories but we will argue that any of these qualities can be developed and nurtured both through training and practice.

Self-assessment questions

Siraj-Blatchford and Clark (2000) offer a very useful framework for self-assessment which you will find helpful in your appraisal of your own equality practice as you prepare your evidence for EYP validation. This can be found at: http://www.multiverse.ac.uk/attachments/be035f1b-ac4f-4b5d-aa1b-3be054bf8f69.doc.

1. In what ways has the position of our wider society in relation to diversity changed over the past 50 years or so? What has been the impact of this change on Early Years practice? (Answer: pages 32–33)

2. Why is the language and terminology relating to diversity so important? (Answer: page 33)

3. What do we need to think about when writing or reviewing policy statements? (Answer: page 35)

4. What do we know about the development of young children's attitudes to diversity (Answer: pages 37–38)

5. Why is the relationship between key person and individual child so crucial in equality practice? (Answer: pages 38–39)

6. What conclusions are being drawn about current inequalities in Early Years service provision from recent Sure Start evaluations and from the Pre-School Learning Alliance? (Answer: pages 40–44)

7. Highlight three of the key messages about equality practice that are emerging from the EYFS framework (Answer: pages 41–42).

FURTHER READING

Lindon, J. (2006) *Equality in Early Childhood: Linking Theory and Practice.* London: Hodder Arnold (Chapters 6 and 7).

Sutherland, M. (2005) *Gifted and Talented in the Early Years.* London: Sage (Chapter 1).

Access the 'All of Us' Inclusion Checklist produced by 'Kids' at http://www.kids.org.uk and the Early Years Equality website at http://www.earlyyearsequality.org, or find these and other resources on the CD-ROM resource with the EYFS framework pack (DCSF, 2008d).

4 The qualities, skills and attributes required for the role of leader of practice

CHAPTER OBJECTIVES

In this chapter, we explore in more detail the essential competences and traits required for the role of leader of practice. As our focus, we take the three generic skills required for the EYP role as identified by CWDC (2007a): decision-making based on sound judgement; attributes of leadership; and communication skills. The dimension of the EYP role as an 'agent of change' (CWDC, 2007a) is explored in depth. You will have an opportunity to use case studies and reflective exercises to support your thinking and to complete an audit of your own strengths and areas for development in these aspects of the role.

After reading this chapter you should be able to:
- reflect on the skills, qualities and attributes required for the role of leader of practice;
- appraise critically your own strengths and areas for development in this area;
- apply your understanding to the preparation of your evidence for EYP validation.

This chapter is wide-ranging and will help you in your preparation of evidence against many of the Standards but focuses particularly on Standards 17, 18, 22, 24, 25, 28, 30, 33, 38 and 39.

Introduction

We have already identified that there is, as yet, no clearly accepted understanding or definition of the 'leader of practice' but a tentative one was offered in Chapter 1 and it is this which is explored more fully in this chapter. We have an emerging definition of the leader of practice, who is able to demonstrate:

- reflective and reflexive practice in her/his own role and skills in decision-making;

- sound knowledge and understanding of Early Years pedagogy: the holistic needs of all children from birth to five and competence in planning, implementing and monitoring within the Early Years Foundation Stage framework (DCSF, 2008a);

- strong values of the intrinsic worth of each child and all those in her/his world;

- the ability to role-model, lead and support others in high quality practice;

- the ability to define a vision for practice within a setting;

- competence as an agent of change.

All Early Years practitioners should demonstrate certain core characteristics: a passion for and strong commitment to quality provision for young children; a flexible approach to practice; the capacity to work independently and as part of a team; skills in caring for, nurturing and teaching young children; patience; sensitivity; and a sense of humour. But in this chapter we focus specifically on the attributes of the leader of practice. Your role in leading the EYFS (DfES, 2007) is explored more fully in the next chapter but some of the other attributes of leadership included in our definition are addressed here, including those relating to decision-making based on sound judgement, effective communication, a clear grasp of the pedagogical role, and visionary leadership as an agent of change. Our discussion begins with consideration of the EYP as a skilled reflective and reflexive practitioner.

The reflective practitioner: key to decision-making based on sound judgement

You may like to look back to Chapter 2 and the work of Boddy et al. (2005) on the role of the social pedagogue. We have identified that we can draw helpful parallels between the characteristics and attributes of the European model of pedagogy and those required for the role of the EYP. The pedagogue should have high expectations of her/himself and others, including the children and staff in the setting. One of the key characteristics of the social pedagogue, highlighted by Boddy et al. (2005), is the ability to reflect critically on her/his own practice and on practice within the setting, with strong self-awareness. Whalley (2005a) refers to this as a key aspect of pedagogical leadership.

For you, then, skilled reflection as part of decision-making based on sound judgement is of crucial importance in preparing evidence to meet the EYP Standards. Indeed, the final two Standards (S38 and S39) focus specifically on these aspects and the strongest evidence is that which identifies your skills in the context of your role in leading practice. How do you show yourself to be a competent reflective practitioner and how do you then enable others to become more reflective in their practice? In particular, how do you demonstrate that you are able to analyse both strengths and areas for development within a setting or particular aspect of practice?

CASE STUDY

Maura, in Task 1 of the written tasks submitted during her final assessment for EYP status, describes and discusses her role in introducing treasure baskets to the baby room in her setting. This was a new aspect of practice to most of the staff team so Maura organised staff training and worked with the team on creating treasure baskets and establishing an appropriate supply of resources to develop these, working with parents and carers to gather these and keep staff informed of the babies' preferences and interests. She modelled the staff role in supporting and observing the babies with the baskets and provided the team with ongoing guidance and practical help. Maura also facilitated a session for corporate reflection and evaluation of the innovation with the staff team

CASE STUDY CONTINUED

around two months after the treasure baskets were introduced. Note how Maura concludes her written report here:

1.6: Your personal learning	Standard
At the beginning of this project when I first introduced the idea and showed the Elenor Goldschmied video to the staff, I was aware that whilst most of them were very enthusiastic about the idea, one member of staff had real concerns about the safety of the babies. She was worried that using so many natural materials and 'from home' resources might be unhygienic and the resources not carry the appropriate safety mark. When I first heard this, I was very dismissive of her attitude and expressed my frustration. Almost immediately, however, I regretted this and realised that my approach was totally inappropriate and quite unprofessional. I apologised to the staff member concerned and invited her to share her concerns in more detail. It turned out that she hadn't understood the role of the adult in heuristic play nor had she heard what I'd said about the importance of keeping resources clean, checking and changing them regularly. In the end, she became one of the most enthusiastic team members and really applied herself to creating a basket for one of her key babies. She wrote some beautiful observations of the baby exploring an egg whisk. Through this, I realised the importance not only of checking that everyone has understood but of taking any concerns seriously and always trying to see the other's view point. In future, I would spend more time before introducing a new idea or aspect of practice trying to analyse and predict some of the negatives as well as the positives.	38 39

REFLECTIVE TASK

How is Maura demonstrating her skills as a reflective and self-aware leader of practice here?

The concept of the reflective practitioner is now well established across the social sciences, thanks to the influence of key figures like John Dewey (1933), Donald Schön (1983) and others; but it is writers such as Hallet (2004), Leeson (2004) and Trodd (2005) who offer specific and practical guidance about reflective practice in an Early Years context. Trodd (2005: 3) describes the reflective Early Years practitioner as '... professional and competent ... continuously seeking to improve (their) practice' and goes on to describe the key component of reflective practice as the capacity to 'think critically'. This includes taking personal responsibility for the way we work with children, families and colleagues, the capacity to work autonomously and to manage change thoughtfully. Reflective leaders show sensitivity to others, drawing on evidence to ensure the validity of their practice now and for the future. This provides a secure base for sound judgement.

In the last chapter, we identified the importance of the EYP having a strong sense of self and a high degree of self-awareness in leading practice. Moyles (2006: 14) reminds us that self-identity cannot be taken as a given but has to be 'achieved and sustained by a process of reflection'.

Brookfield's approach to critical reflection includes the suggestion that we look at reality through 'four critical lenses: our own viewpoint; our colleagues' viewpoint; the viewpoint of the learners; and the viewpoint offered by theoretical literature' (Brookfield, 1995, cited in Trodd, 2005: 4). Arguably, these four perspectives will result in well-informed judgements.

Leeson (2004: 149) suggests that one of the most useful models for reflection in Early Years practice is that offered by Ghaye and Ghaye (1998) which highlights different levels of reflection:

- **descriptive** – giving an account of the incident;

- **perceptive** – making links between the description and one's own feelings;

- **receptive** – allowing ourselves to be open to different perspectives on the account;

- **interactive** – creating links between one's learning here and future action;

- **critical** – questioning accepted practice in a creative and constructive manner, developing new theories and ways of working for oneself and others.

Hallet (2004) breaks this down into simple question format, suggesting that essentially, the reflective practitioner needs to be self-questioning. As you apply the leadership skills required for the EYP role, you should also encourage other practitioners to ask of themselves:

- What kind of practitioner am I?

- What kind of practitioner do I want to be?

- How do the children view me?

- How do my colleagues view me?

- How do the parents view me?

- How do I want others to see me?

(Based on Hallet, 2004: 48)

REFLECTIVE TASK

Think of a routine activity that is part of your current role – such as reading stories to children, supporting their care needs (feeding; changing etc.), engaging with them in outdoor play, etc. Use the questions above to reflect on the type of practitioner you are and/or would like to be. How do you know how others perceive you?

By reflecting not only on policy and practice but on the way we carry out our roles and others' perceptions of us, we are able to analyse whether things are as they should be or whether changes are needed and to base these on sound judgement. Reflective dialogue (Anning and Edwards, 2006) is a core component of this and includes constructive discussion with key others, especially colleagues. Thus, it becomes the 'vehicle for knowledge exchange and joint knowledge construction' (Anning and Edwards, 2006: 149) There are strong grounds to understand this as a key part of the role of the leader of practice, especially in decision-making. Indeed, this underpins EYP S33 where you should demonstrate that you can: 'establish and sustain a culture of collaborative and cooperative working between colleagues' (CWDC, 2007a: 9.) This goes way beyond the leadership aspect of 'mentoring' (Rodd, 2006) which we discuss later in the book, because at the heart of reflective dialogue is mutual learning.

REFLECTIVE TASK

(A critical friend), is a person who asks provocative questions, provides data to be examined through another lens, and offers critiques of a person's work as a friend . . . taking time to understand the context of the work presented and the outcome that the person . . . is working towards.

(Costa and Kallick, 1993: 50)

As part of your preparation for EYP validation, you may identify someone to act as 'critical friend' for you. Think now, though, of who acts in this role generally for your work as leader of practice. How important is this in helping you see practice through a range of lenses? How does this support your leadership role?

The fourth lens identified by Brookfield (1995) is the lens of the theoretical literature. Alongside personal reflection and reflective dialogue, the EYP demonstrates herself to be one who can integrate knowledge into practice, particularly in decision-making, using the theories and literature that are available to demonstrate the application of theory to real experience. Indeed, Ghaye and Ghaye (1998: 3) refer to reflection as 'practice with principle.'

REFLECTIVE TASK

Think of two examples of how you have made strong connections between your understanding of relevant theory or something you have read and your practice. What decisions did you make? .How do these examples exemplify your skills in reaching sound judgements and as a leader of practice?

The EYP as agent of change

As human beings we may have an ambivalent attitude to change. We tend to be both resistant to it and at the same time strangely impelled by it. Change and adaptation have been crucial for human survival, and within organisations, too, informed change is essential for success. Change, then, is both an inevitable and necessary part of our lives as individuals, professionally and within wider society. This is not to imply an approach that embraces change without any critical thought but it does highlight the need for an openness to new ways of understanding and of 'doing' practice. In the EYP role, you will need to model a positive but intelligent attitude to changes to practice, to understand some of the underlying causes of resistance to change and to apply some of the principles of change management to your role as an agent of change.

From her research, Rodd (2006) identifies a variety of types of change at different levels in early childhood settings: incremental, induced, routine, crisis, innovative and trans-formational. As an EYP, you may be involved with any one of these but the focus of your leadership role lies in induced and innovative change. Induced change stems from a conscious decision that some aspect of practice relating to people or processes needs to be changed; for instance, the reorganisation of a key person system in a setting. In innovative change, the leader seeks to introduce new practices in order to further the overall mission of a setting, such as changes to the way a programme is planned, using the children's own interests rather than a thematic approach.

One of the most determining success factors in the implementation of change is the level of support or resistance from the staff involved. Why do some people demonstrate such resistance and appear to sabotage projects or planned change? There are many complex reasons including misunderstandings of the purpose, lack of trust in the leader, lack of knowledge, fear of new technologies, ideological factors (differing personal stances about Early Years practice), lack of shared ownership, experience of excessive change and self-interest (based on Rodd, 2006: 189). In order to support staff in the change process, the following six 'C's of change are suggested (Schrag et al., 1985, cited in Rodd, 2006):

- **challenge:** aim to creatively turn perceived 'threats' into a positive challenge;
- **communication:** consult widely and regularly with all staff keeping them informed throughout the process;
- **commitment/collaboration:** encourage shared ownership of the change and try to avoid any suggestion that this is being 'imposed';
- **control:** allow all staff to feel that they are sharing in control of shape and pace of any change;
- **confidence:** encourage resilience and self-confidence in staff;
- **connection:** promote networks of support, both within a setting and from outside agencies where helpful.

REFLECTIVE TASK

Can you think of examples of both induced and innovative change in which you have led practice? From the six 'C's above, are you able to identify factors that contributed to either the success or lack of success in supporting this change?

The agent of change as 'creative leader'

We might add a further 'C' to Schrag et al.'s list. The effective agent of change needs to be a *creative* leader. As Edgington states (2004: 8), the leader with creativity and imagination will demonstrate an 'optimistic disposition . . . a 'can do' approach', showing that with ingenuity and persistence anything can be made to happen. The leader of practice has to be a 'possibility thinker', willing to *un*learn the tendency to follow conventional patterns and make predictable responses and develop innovative but workable approaches to all aspects of practice. This will involve the 'integration of your *expertise* and *experience* in order to bring a creative approach to problem-solving' (Isaksen and Tidd, 2006: 142); and to hold your professional expertise with your professional experience in balanced tension. Such an approach requires creative intelligence. It includes navigating change to ensure its successful achievement rather than resulting in acrimony or failure. More than this, when you apply creative intelligence to your leadership role you are providing the energy to overcome any inertia within your colleagues or setting.

CASE STUDY

When Alison, lead practitioner in the pre-school room of a private nursery, wanted to introduce greater flexibility to snack time for the children and create a self-service system whereby children could select when they had a snack, she met with a lot of resistance from the staff team. They insisted the present system worked well: it was a fixed focal point to the session, was used as a social occasion with key children and ensured that every child did indeed have their snack. From Alison's value stance, however, the present system was intrusive and the children had to stop in the middle of play situations and come to the tables. She carried out some observations to back this up and shared these with the staff. Alison then used a team meeting to outline the rationale for and details of her vision for snack time and appealed to the staff to introduce the system two days a week for a month and then meet again to review. Alison outlined that the social dimension would not be lost and encouraged staff to be vigilant to how the children used the new self-service area and to join their key children at the table whenever possible. At the end of the month, the staff had seen for themselves that the children's play was no longer disrupted and offered positive feedback to Alison about how the new system had enabled them to have quality time with some of their key children during snack time.

REFLECTIVE TASK

Identify ways in which Alison balanced her professional expertise here with the importance of working with the staff team and all their concerns (experience). Why was she so successful here? Can you think of an opportunity you have had to balance your expertise with your current experience?

We see here again the concept of the Early Years setting as 'a 'community of learners' and Isaksen and Tidd (2006: 143) remind us that creative leadership involves 'intense learning' for the leader as well as those being led. This involves adding *new* knowledge to existing expertise and experience, an openness to new ways of thinking and a solution-focused approach to all the challenges of practice. This involves a high degree of emotional resilience and the need to be resourceful and imaginative in the approach taken.

CASE STUDY

Bev is the leader of a voluntary pre-school on the edge of a large city. The group meets in the large hall of a local church which is on the first floor and accommodation comprises one large and two small base rooms with kitchen and toilet facilities. There is no provision for using outdoors as the church car park is not secure and, in any case, is used constantly throughout the week. Once a week, the staff would clear the large base room and the children would have opportunity for activities involving whole body coordination on a climbing frame etc and/or in movement play.

As Bev reflected on this pattern, she became increasingly dissatisfied and consulted with colleagues, parents, children and other professionals. Bev led their collective thinking of a creative solution: one of the smaller rooms was developed into a permanent 'movement room' with a range of different resources set out and activities planned there on a daily basis, including obstacle courses etc., to which the children had free-flow access. Observations showed that the children were able to have much greater control of their own learning under this new arrangement.

REFLECTIVE TASK

How does Bev apply creative leadership in this situation? Can you think of two examples when you have used a similarly creative approach to leadership in your own setting?

The agent of change as 'visionary leader'

Leaders should be visionary yet realistic; sensitive but demanding, innovative yet practical.

(Smith and Langston, 1999: 20)

We have noted previously Rodd's (2006) and Moyles' (2006) work on defining the role of the leader as visionary and influential. Clearly, the ability to define and articulate a vision for practice within your Early Years setting is a crucial aspect of your EYP leadership role. Your vision will stem from your personal value stance, information and personal reflections on the direction of travel of Early Years policy, your personal commitment to your own learning, your wider reading of the theoretical literature and your contextual knowledge of your immediate setting. Each of these aspects is important. As part of your role as 'visionary leader' you will introduce to practice any necessary *information* and *expertise* from this wider context.

CASE STUDY

Georgia is the manager of a full day nursery. As such she is usually the first point of contact for the setting: for parents, other professionals and statutory bodies etc. Over recent months, Georgia has been involved in leading practice on improving the nursery's approach to:

- *planning for the under-threes;*

- *introducing a healthy eating menu;*

- *creating a more effective system of free-flow movement for children in the nursery environment (indoors and out);*

- *behaviour management, including encouraging the children to create their own ground rules;*

- *communication with parents through the establishing of open afternoons at weekends with emphasis on a particular aspect of learning/development – such as communication, language and literacy;*

- *staff's competence in using ICT to support teaching and learning.*

REFLECTIVE TASK

All these are aspects of practice, so although Georgia also has primary responsibility for organisation in her setting, she is also the lead practitioner. Think about the information and expertise that Georgia has needed in order to lead on these. Begin to reflect on the way you access key information and acquire the expertise required for you to lead change in your own setting.

Walden and Shiba (2001) outline eight principles for the visionary leader and whilst not all these are directly applicable to the role of EYP they do offer some important insights into the role, especially in leading change. Their principles are adapted here with some reflective questions to offer you a tool with which you can appraise your own role.

REFLECTIVE TASK

Table 4.1 Principles of visionary practice

Walden and Shiba's (2001) Principles of visionary leadership	Application to your own leadership practice
Principle 1 The visionary leader is observant and vigilant and must do on-site observation leading to personal perception of changes in societal values.	In what ways do you act as a conduit of key information relating to policy and practice matters in your setting?
EYP role: Here the role of the leader in empowering staff by keeping them fully informed of key changes affecting policy and practice is emphasised. This includes staff changing their own perceptions and value stance.	

Principle 2 Even though there is resistance, the visionary leader never gives up; squeezing the resistance between outside-in pressure in combination with top-down inside instruction.

EYP role: Here the often precarious role of the leader in translating and making many of the changes 'manageable' and 'doable' to/by staff is stressed.

Can you think of an instance when your vision for practice was met with resistance by colleagues? What helped you to stick with your vision here?

Principle 3 The visionary leader begins transformation of practice with symbolic disruption of the old or traditional system through top-down efforts to create chaos within the organisation.

EYP role: The role of the leader is being able to deal positively and effectively with the chaos that is an inevitable part of transition from one way of organising/ 'doing' practice and another.

Think of an instance when you have been involved in leading change to practice. What personal coping strategies do you have to enable you to cope with the chaos of transition and retain your sense of vision?

Principle 4 The direction of visionary transformation is illustrated by a symbolic visible image and the visionary leader's symbolic behaviour.

EYP role: We will address this further in Chapters 6 and 7 but shared action planning and positive role-modelling by the leader – not just by action but by attitude – are crucial factors in successful visionary transformation.

Think further of the instance above. How did you convey by both action and attitude your positive approach to change?

Principle 5 Quickly establishing new physical, organisational and behavioural systems is essential for successful visionary transformation.

EYP role: This principle needs a note of caution! The management and timing of change are critical. New systems *are* indeed crucial but what is needed of the leader is to inspire confidence in colleagues and to empower them to play their part in implementing change. Getting the timing/timescale for this 'right' is a key leadership skill.

What organisational skills do you believe you bring to visionary leadership? Are there any you particularly need to develop? Can you think back to the time management aspect of the instance above? In retrospect, reflect on the appropriateness of this.

Principle 6 Real change leaders are necessary to enable transformation.

EYP role: Skills in change management are essential for all leaders of practice. This is addressed more fully in Chapter 6.

Begin to reflect on your skills and areas for development in change management

Principle 7 Create an innovative system to provide feedback from results.

EYP role: In order to continuously encourage and support colleagues in changes to practice, it is important to build in regular opportunities for feedback, review and updates.

Think of the last time you created an action plan with colleagues in order to implement some aspect of change to practice. Did this include structured opportunity for review on a regular basis? If not, why not?

Principle 8 Create a daily operation system, including a new work structure, new approach to human capabilities and improvement activities.

EYP role: This connects to the role of EYP as leading reflective practitioner, encouraging colleagues to review their own practice and engage in an ongoing programme of continuing professional development (CPD).

How do you share with colleagues your own programme of CPD? In what ways do you role-model effective reflective practice on a daily basis?

I have needed to show vision, determination, resilience and commitment as I prepared for EYP validation.

(Janine, EYP)

Personal communication skills

One of the most critical elements in effective leadership is that of interpersonal skills. We will consider the quality required of an effective leader more comprehensively in Chapter 6 when we focus on the teamwork elements of leadership but here we focus on the personal: on the individual skills and attributes which are so important for leadership of practice. We have already identified that leaders in early childhood are predominantly women. Indeed, it can be argued that the development of the Early Years profession has been shaped to a large extent by the position of women in society (Ebbeck and Waniganayake, 2003). Historically, this is reflected in the low pay and status of Early Years (mainly female) practitioners. It is worth reminding ourselves, however, that many of the early pioneers of quality childcare practice and provision were strong, determined women

– such as Maria Montessori (1870–1952), Margaret McMillan (1860–1931) and Susan Isaacs (1885–1948) and that the majority of leading contemporary writers on Early Years are women.

Leadership and gender

Rodd (2006: 31–4) offers a useful critique of leadership and gender, though there is a risk of over-simplification here. She argues that the traditional model of leadership is considered to be more male in orientation and is characterised by control, power, domination and competition. A study in the 1970s by Hennig and Jardim (cited in Rodd, 2006) suggests that the attributes of a feminine model of leadership would contrast greatly with these 'male' characteristics and would focus on relationships, consensus, collaboration and flexibility.

Interestingly, research by Kinney in 1992 (cited in Rodd 2006) suggests that in early childhood settings, there is no measurable difference in the actual *functions* of leadership carried out by men or women and the essential tasks remain the same regardless of the leader's gender. These are empowering, restructuring, taking responsibility for teaching and learning, acting as a role model and being open and questioning about all aspects of practice. However, Kinney's research did highlight the fact that the *style* of leadership demonstrated by women and men differs. Women generally use a facilitating style and men a more authoritarian approach (Whalley, 2002).

Paradoxically, while the glass ceiling remains a real barrier to aspiring women leaders in many professions, the great majority of EYPs to date are women and – although beyond the remit of this publication – we face the significant challenge of encouraging more men to pursue careers in Early Years practice to counterbalance the perceived 'feminised' culture by which it is characterised. Indeed, there is an important sense of growing empowerment among many women leaders in Early Years settings but, for both women and men, leadership in the Early Years is clearly to follow a facilitating model:

> The future of management is 'female' with the feminine attributes of cooperation, communication, diplomacy and insight preferred over the traditional male attributes of competition, aggression, hierarchy and logic.
>
> *(Grant, cited in Rodd, 2006: 31)*

CASE STUDY

Ken *is a popular leader of the pre-school room in a children's centre, with a collaborative style of working. He exhibits none of the 'traditional male attributes' described above. Indeed, his female colleagues all consider him 'one of them' and there is generally very effective teamwork in the base room.*

Linda, *by contrast, is the supervisor of a pre-school group in her local village. She has worked in the setting for 18 years and is a forceful character who has definite ideas about* *how the group should be organised and run and who adopts a fairly authoritarian style with her staff. The management committee, mainly parents, are very much in awe of her and generally allow her to have her way.*

REFLECTIVE TASK

Ken and Linda remind us that we do need to guard against gender stereotyping but Cox (1996) suggests that women have an instinctive antipathy towards leadership roles involving authority and power and this has affected the way leadership in early childhood has evolved. Are you aware of this in your own experience? What effect do you think this has had on the way Early Years settings are run? Can you identify core features of leadership of practice that transcend gender?

Assertive leadership

Fundamentally, as a leader of Early Years practice, you will need to have a high level of self-esteem and to value greatly your role and the overall place and contribution of effective Early Years practice to wider society. Furthermore, from healthy self-esteem will come appropriate self-assertion: the skill to convey calmly, competently and confidently your own feelings (positive and negative), opinions, beliefs and needs in such a way that does not negatively affect the self-esteem of anyone else (Dryden and Constantinou, 2004). Of course, the reality is much more challenging than the rhetoric. But with healthy self-awareness will come understanding of situations or people to which/whom you behave and respond passively, aggressively or manipulatively rather than assertively. As a leader of practice, you have significant responsibility in role-modelling an assertive approach to your colleagues.

PRACTICAL TASK

Use the following scenarios to identify if the leader in question is responding/ communicating passively, aggressively, or manipulatively. In the right hand column, identify a more appropriately assertive response.

Table 4.2 Leadership responses

Scenario	Type of response	Alternative appropriate assertive response
Carla, a childminder, fails to make eye contact with a parent who is late collecting her baby for the third day running. Carla is non-communicative to the parent, merely handing over the child's bag.		
Pete works in a Sure Start local project and ignores a negative comment he overhears from a parent that men shouldn't work in Early Years settings.		
Claudette is lead practitioner of the baby room in a private nursery. She shouts at one of her members of staff who has failed to dispose of a child's nappy in an appropriate way.		
Morna is a lead practitioner in a children's centre. When one of the parents raises a significant concern about practice in the nursery, Morna uses self-disclosure to share some of her own pressing domestic issues.		
Kezia is supervisor of a pre-school. A student on placement spends a lot of time with one child, reading one book after another to him. Kezia storms into the book area, takes the book off the student and states: 'That's enough!'		

A consistently assertive communication style remains one to which most of us can only aspire but within the EYP role. It is important that you cultivate a self-assured approach in a variety of situations where you have opportunity to lead approach and try and avoid the pitfalls of either passivity or aggression.

C H A P T E R   S U M M A R Y

In this chapter, we have identified some of the essential traits, characteristics and qualities required by the EYP in the role of leader of practice. In particular, skills in reflective practice that are key to effective decision-making and skills in leading change using creative and visionary leadership styles have been highlighted. While you have reflected on your own personal skills and attributes, as a competent and confident communicator, through the case studies offered and other exercises, you may well have begun a personal skills audit. At the end of the chapter you are encouraged to formalise this. This all connects very clearly with EYP S38 and S39 where any approaches to innovation or changes to practice must be supported with skilled reflection and analysis both of the situation and of your own role. As leaders of practice, a confident and assertive approach to your role should be accompanied by healthy awareness that as a leader you are also a learner.

Moving on

In the next chapter, the focus moves from the skills/attributes of leadership to the many specific roles required of the EYP. In particular, the role of the EYP in leading change and introducing and implementing legislation is addressed. This includes the challenges and opportunities of leading the Early Years Foundation Stage.

Self-assessment: personal skills audit

In this chapter the self-assessment task is not so much a 'test' of how much factual information you have assimilated, but rather it offers you opportunity to formalise your reflections and to identify both your own strengths and areas for development. You can then devise an action plan to show how you might address any areas for development. When planning action, think about the following:

- **Prioritising:** Which of the areas highlighted for development needs to be addressed immediately/in the medium term/long term?

- **Aims/intentions:** What exactly are you aiming for? It is important to spend time clarifying this at the outset.

- **Support:** The role of a critical friend and mentor is important here but equally who else in the setting do you need to support you as you address this area?

- **Resources:** Is there a training programme you might access? A course of further study or training you might join? Books or other resources for purchase? What about budget implications here?

- **Criteria for success**: How will you know you've achieved your aim?

- **Review**: Any action – personal or organisational – needs to be reviewed and a date should be set for this initial review at the outset.

Table 4.3   Personal skills audit

SELF AUDIT:

Skills/Attributes	Experience (in current or previous setting)	Personal strengths	Areas for development	Action points
High expectations of self, children and colleagues (page 52)				
Autonomy and personal responsibility/accountability (pages 53–54)				
Reflective dialogue with colleagues (page 55).				
Willingness to engage with a professional critical friend (page 55).				
Creativity (page 57)				
Self-assertiveness (page 64)				
Vision (pages 60–62)				

ACTION PLAN:

Action needed	Aims/intentions	Time scale	People involved	Resources/cost implications	Criteria for success	Date for review

Leeson, C. (2007) In praise of reflective practice. In Willan, J., Parker-Rees, R. and Savage, J. *Early Childhood Studies* (2nd edn). Exeter: Learning Matters.

Rodd, J. (2006) Initiating and implementing change. In *Leadership in Early Childhood* (3rd edn). Buckingham: Open University Press.

5 Meeting the challenges of leading practice

CHAPTER OBJECTIVES

In this chapter we reflect on different priorities that an Early Years Professional (EYP) will need to address when developing effective practice. You will explore the implementation of change, particularly change which applies to policy and procedures inherent in the Early Years Foundation Stage (EYFS) framework (DCSF, 2008a). Activities and reflective tasks will enable you to consider influential factors that you will encounter as you take on the challenge of leading practice.

After reading this chapter you should be able to:
- reflect on how you manage different priorities that promote enhanced outcomes for children and families;
- explore ways of leading practice through implementing policies and procedures;
- develop an awareness of some of the challenges encountered when implementing the EYFS and recognise opportunities to manage these issues effectively.

This chapter will help you to reflect on all of the Standards for EYPs (CWDC, 2007a). The groups of Standards interlink, so an awareness of the connections between the groups will enable you to explore the many factors involved in leading practice.

Introduction

Early Years Professionals will be key to raising the quality of early years provision. They will be change agents to lead practice. They will be expected to lead practice across the EYFS in a range of settings, modelling the skills and behaviours that promote good outcomes for children.

(CWDC, 2007a: 4)

As we have already seen, the recent expansion of services within the Early Years sector has been accompanied by a determination to enhance the quality of Early Years provision. The EYFS framework (DCSF, 2008a) is rooted in *Choice for Parents, the Best Start for Children: A Ten Year Strategy for Childcare* (HM Treasury, 2004) and the Childcare Act 2006 is central to Government policy for improving outcomes for all children.

Statutory from September 2008, the EYFS framework provides very clear principles for all settings to adopt and for leaders of practice to promote; it is the common thread linking the diverse nature of Early Years settings and local community needs that forms the backdrop to your role of leading practice. As an EYP, you will be expected to lead practice across the EYFS and support others to 'deliver personalised learning, development and care to help children to get the best possible start in life' (DCSF, 2008b: 6). In this chapter, you will have an opportunity to reflect on some of the priorities that need to be considered when undertaking this significant role. For example, you will examine the implications of both internal and external policies and compliance with Ofsted requirements.

The challenges that you will encounter in your role of leading practice require the application of wide-ranging knowledge and skills. Specific attributes of a leader of practice were identified in the previous chapter. Here, we explore how to embark on implementing policies and procedures within the context of your Early Years setting and to tackle the challenges implicit in your role as an agent of change (CWDC, 2007a). This chapter adopts a structured approach, based on the four guiding themes of the EYFS: a unique child, positive relationships, enabling environments, and learning and development, which all work together to underpin effective practice. It is important to recognise that the themes are not mutually exclusive and must be viewed holistically when tackling opportunities to effectively implement and develop the framework in your setting.

The EYFS framework adopts a principled approach to fulfil its overarching aim, which is to help young children achieve the five outcomes for *Every Child Matters*: 'staying safe', 'being healthy', 'enjoying and achieving', 'making a positive contribution', and 'achieving economic well-being' (DfES, 2003). Within the four guiding themes of the EYFS, there are four guiding principles to consider and these are stated at the beginning of each section. The various principles provide a starting point for you to explore the challenges of leading effective practice. You should also refer to the four commitments that support each principle in the EYFS framework: these commitments express how you might apply the principles to your practice.

Theme 1: a unique child

Every child is a competent learner from birth who can be resilient, capable, confident and self-assured.

(DCSF, 2008a)

Child development, inclusive practice, keeping safe, and health and well-being are the commitments that support the principle provided above for Theme 1: a unique child (DCSF, 2008a). Running throughout all the EYFS themes, the child at the centre of practice is a principle that stands alongside the conviction that we can only begin fully to understand the factors influencing each individual child's development when we engage with each family's story and its unique set of circumstances.

The EYFS Welfare Requirements provide the 'general and specific legal requirements' (DCSF, 2008a: 20) that each Early Years setting must adhere to in order to create the kind of environment where children can thrive. To be able to focus effectively on meeting the needs of individual children, EYPs must also have a secure understanding of the policy context within which they work. Standard 5 for EYPS emphasises the need for leaders of practice to understand fully 'the current legal requirements, national policies and guidance on health and safety, safeguarding and promoting the well-being of children and their implications for Early Years settings' (CWDC, 2007a: 19).

REFLECTIVE TASK

EYFS Welfare Requirement 'Safeguarding and promoting children's welfare' (DCSF, 2008a) is broken down into a number of headings:

Safeguarding, Information and Complaints, Premises and Security, Outings, Equality of Opportunities, Medicines, Illnesses and Injuries, Food and Drink, Smoking and Behaviour Management.

Select one of the above and look at the policy you have in place in your setting and the procedures you have adopted to address this aspect of safeguarding and promoting children's welfare. Ask yourself the following questions.

1 Do I really understand the legal requirements relating to this policy?

2 Am I fully aware of any local guidelines that are in place?

3 Have I consulted with other professionals who could offer additional expertise or guidance?

4 Have I given other practitioners the opportunity to contribute their ideas and engage with the intentions of the policy?

5 To what extent have I involved parents and children?

6 Is the policy an effective working document?

Local authorities are required under the Childcare Act 2006 'to reduce inequalities and improve the well-being of all young children in their area' (DCSF, 2007a: 6). Well-being in this context is defined by the five *Every Child Matters* outcomes and includes the emphasis in the EYFS that 'children's health is an integral part of their emotional, mental, social, environmental and spiritual well-being' (DCSF, 2007c: Principles into Practice [PiP] 1.4). One of the challenges facing you as a leader of practice is to find ways of implementing the EYFS Welfare Requirements (DCSF, 2008a) showing that you are well informed by the wider policy agenda as well as remaining responsive to the specific needs of the children and families within your local community and the context of your setting (Draper and Duffy, 2006).

Ofsted's role is not only to ensure that each setting is meeting the statutory requirements of the EYFS in providing quality care and early education, but also to 'judge how well providers organise their childcare to help promote children's well-being' (Ofsted, 2008).

'What is it like for a child here?'(Ofsted, 2008) is the question inspectors will have in mind when they come to inspect your setting. Recent legislation, the Childcare Act 2006 in particular, places additional emphasis on this question by including a requirement for local authorities to 'have regard to the views of young children aged from birth to 5 in discharging their duties in relation to early childhood services' (McAuliffe et al., 2006: 22). Following on from this, one of the priorities for practice is expressed in EYPS Standard 27: 'Listen to children, pay attention to what they say and value and respect their views' (CWDC, 2007a). In your role as an EYP, the challenge is to:

- find ways to include **all** children;

- pay close attention to the individual ways children have of communicating their thoughts, feelings and intentions;

- provide time and space for children to make their own choices and decisions;

- realise that the way children play and behave is a form of communication;

- provide play opportunities and materials so that children can contribute their views in different ways;

- let children know that their views are important by giving them feedback;

- let children see that their views are important by making changes that they have contributed to;

- check with children that you have represented their views accurately;

- be aware that all practitioners are influenced by their personal values, histories and circumstances which can interfere with their ability to listen to children.

(Adapted from Lancaster, 2006)

REFLECTIVE TASK

The following extract is from an observation of a 9 month old baby who is exploring a treasure basket:

> *His eyes rest on a large blue stone. He picks up the large stone with his right hand and turns it over on his lap using both hands. Still using both hands he picks the stone up and begins to bite it, making a noise as his teeth grind against the hard surface. He smiles, looking at his mother as he repeatedly bites the stone over and over again. He stops, holds the stone up to his face and looks at it intently then puts it to his mouth once again.*

> *(Nutbrown and Clough, 2006: 76–7)*

The 'Reflecting on Practice' section from the 'Child Development' PiP card 1.1 (DCSF, 2007c) suggests that it is important to think about each child's 'unique development, individual interests, communication style and learning style'. The observation above provides us with the opportunity to listen to this particular baby and reflect on what he is communicating to us.

REFLECTIVE TASK CONTINUED

Using the bullet points above about different ways of listening to children:

- *identify how you 'listen' to children in your setting;*

- *explore with colleagues how you might improve on this aspect of practice.*

'When you are trying to identify problems that may affect a child's welfare, it is necessary to have a clear understanding of the generic processes involved in babies' and young children's growth, development and learning and in depth knowledge of each child's 'unique development' (DCSF, 2007c: PiP 1.1). Recording information about children's progress or incidents causing concern is another aspect of your practice that is of vital importance, especially when information needs to be communicated to parents or other professionals (Wall, 2006). Sharing information with other professionals and organisations is an important element of multi-agency working, which is a key aspect of the Government's drive to improve the outcomes for children and is increasingly relevant for all practitioners. Balancing the need for accurate and up-to-date paperwork with active listening and responding to children is a concern expressed by practitioners and is a challenge which needs to be acknowledged by leaders of practice (Jones, 2004).

It is important to work together so that difficulties arising from competing demands can be tackled and shared and appropriate solutions can be found. This kind of working culture has an enormous impact on the capacity of staff teams and individual practitioners to focus on the needs of each 'unique child'. It also affects their personal motivation to develop their practice as 'if we do not feel valued by those with whom we work, it is very difficult to decentre from our own concerns and value children and their families' (Moylett and Djemli, 2005: 62).

Theme 2: positive relationships

Children learn to be strong and independent from a base of loving and secure relationships with parents and/or a key person.

(DCSF, 2008a)

Establishing meaningful, positive relationships with children, families, colleagues and other professionals is central to the role of the EYP and underpins all four themes of the EYFS. The commitments for Theme 2, respecting each other, parents as partners, supporting learning, and key person, will help you to focus on these important relationships from different angles so that priorities for practice can be clearly identified. Positive relationships are established through effective communication and good practice requires us to begin to understand each other through different forms of shared communication. As Bruce (2004: 69) explains, 'We use words and signs to do this, but we also communicate with our body language and gestures, the sounds and movements we make, and the way we pause and are silent'.

REFLECTIVE TASK

Look at the PiP cards for 'Theme 2: positive relationships' in the EYFS pack. Read the section on 'effective practice' for each of the cards and then look at the EYPS standards. Make a list of standards which relate to each of the commitments.

Table 5.1 EYFS commitments and EYPS standards

EYFS commitments	EYPS standards
2.1 Respecting each other	
2.2 Parents as partners	
2.3 Supporting learning	
2.4 Key person	

From this reflective task, you should have noticed the emphasis on establishing 'fair, respectful, trusting, supportive and constructive relationships' and communicating 'sensitively and effectively' with both children and parents in S25, S26 and S30 as well as the expectation in S33 to 'establish and sustain a culture of collaborative and cooperative working between colleagues' (CWDC, 2007a).

The key person relationship is an aspect of provision which addresses these Standards; it is pivotal to effective practice and becomes statutory within EYFS provision (DCSF, 2008a). There is agreement from different psychological perspectives that close, consistent relationships with familiar adults are essential for the emotional well being of babies and young children (Elfer et al., 2003, Gerhardt, 2004). *The Birth to Three Matters* framework (DfES, 2002) made reference to the role of the key person from this point of view but the EYFS Practice Guidance (DCSF, 2008b) takes this much further and puts the role firmly at the centre of good practice for all children from 0 to 5 years. There is an understanding that children will have different attachment needs at different stages of development and that 'even when children are older and can hold key people from home in mind for longer, there is still a need for them to have a key person to depend on in the setting' (DCSF, 2008b: 15). The following list highlights some of the benefits of establishing a key person approach.

For children:

- a familiar, trusting adult to rely on;

- an adult who knows them well and can understand their needs;

- an affectionate relationship with an adult in the setting to complement the experience they have at home;

- someone who can hold them in mind and provide them with a sense of belonging.

For parents:

- a familiar person to contact within the setting who is interested in them;

- someone who can share their enjoyment or concerns as the child grows and develops;

- confidence gained from establishing a relationship with the practitioner who spends time with their child.

For the key person:

- getting to know a child and family really well;

- establishing a working partnership with the family for the benefit of the child;

- observing and reflecting on the progress of a child over a period of time;

- the satisfaction of making a difference to the child's holistic development.

For the setting:

- staff who are clearer about their role and feel more involved;

- parents who are more likely to engage in their children's learning;

- greater opportunity for the setting and the family to work together to share a common approach to meeting the child's needs;

- a higher profile for the setting within the local community. (Adapted from Elfer et al., 2003: 18–19).

The challenge in terms of practice is to find ways of implementing the key person approach to meet the specific needs of the children, parents and staff within the context of your own setting. The case study below looks at some of the issues facing an EYP as she explores how to lead and support the staff team to put a key person approach in place.

CASE STUDY

Marija, an EYP in a private nursery

Marija has just started work as an EYP in a large private day nursery taking children between the ages of three months and five years. Most of the parents work full-time and there is little ongoing contact with them apart from occasional evening meetings to discuss the progress of the children. At a recent staff meeting Marija introduced the idea of establishing a key person approach as outlined in the Practice Guidance for the EYFS (DCSF, 2008b). She realised that although children were allocated a named practitioner when they started at the nursery there was very little understanding amongst the staff of the role of a key person and how such an approach could be beneficial to children, parents and staff.

Her suggestion was not met with much enthusiasm by the staff. The team leaders from the baby and toddler rooms were familiar with the role of the key person but had found it

---

---

very difficult to put into practice due to constant staff changes and the problem of organising staff rotas and shifts to coincide with their key children's attendance patterns. Other members of staff expressed the view that it was not good for the children to get too used to one member of staff because they could not always be there. They said how difficult and upsetting it was for them as well as the children when the key person was either busy or out of the room. They felt that it actually made it harder to get on with their work. The remaining practitioners who worked in the pre-school room were dismissive of the need to alter the way they worked to include a key person approach with the older children as they felt that they managed well without one.

Marija knew that an important part of leading practice was to help the staff team come together and share a common purpose (Siraj-Blatchford and Manni, 2007; Rodd, 2006) so she decided to organise a series of staff meetings on the key person approach. She had introduced a system in her previous setting where two members of staff shared a group of key children so that there was always the opportunity for one familiar member of staff to be available by working on the opposite shift from her co-worker. She knew from her previous experience and from her background reading that putting in place a key person approach would in time improve staff morale by making their jobs more satisfying (Elfer et al., 2003).

Now complete the task below:

- *Make a list of the concerns that the practitioners in Marija's setting have about implementing a key person approach.*

- *Look at the resource index from the CD-ROM in the EYFS framework pack (DCSF, 2008d) and open the section on Positive Relationships. Read the document entitled 'Key Person: Effective Practice' and plan the next staff meeting for Marija so that she can address the concerns of the staff.*

In the case study above you have explored some of the challenges from the point of view of the staff team. Goldschmied and Jackson (2004: 203) draw attention to the feelings of parents, particularly mothers, who may experience the relationship their child has with the key person as a threat and 'worry that the child will come to prefer the key person.' These emotional factors are a reality. Although 'encouraging a baby or toddler to develop a close relationship with their key person does not lessen the love between the child and their parents' (Manning-Morton and Thorp, 2003: 33), the feelings of both parents and staff have to be acknowledged and processed.

The key person approach is a good base on which to build when looking at ways of working together to engage parents in the learning and development needs of their children. Parents have specialised knowledge of their individual child and therefore have much to share. When this is combined with the expertise of a professional who has specialised knowledge of early childhood development and learning, then each child can be supported in a holistic way (Athey, 2007). There will inevitably be times when parents and practitioners struggle to come to a shared understanding, particularly in relation to different cultural practices or views on raising children, but this can be overcome in an environment where individual differences are seen as an opportunity rather than a threat (Powell, 2005).

REFLECTIVE TASK

Look at the section on 'Challenges and Dilemmas' from the 'Parents as Partners' PiP card 2.2 (DCSF, 2007c) The first issue raises the question of 'how to get fathers involved'. One way of approaching this challenge is to find ways of helping fathers to tune into their child's interests through a strength they have themselves. The following example is from a children's centre:

A local musician was engaged to set up a father's band recording nursery rhymes and songs, successfully attracting men who would not otherwise have been involved, drawn by the carrot of the professional music recording. The fathers also constructed toys for a nursery rhyme box and planned to develop a sports club alongside their children at a local football club. (Warin, 2007: 94)

Each setting is different and will have its own set of priorities for building positive relationships with parents.

- *What is the main challenge for you in your setting regarding building partnerships with the parents?*

- *Make a list of possible ways to tackle the challenge and discuss your thoughts with colleagues. Explore what action you can take to make improvements.*

Theme 3: enabling environments

The environment plays a key role in supporting and extending children's development and learning.

(DCSF, 2008a)

As you explore Theme 3, you will consider how you can improve the emotional and physical environment in which the child is situated. The commitments for this theme: observation, assessment and planning; supporting every child; and the learning environment and the wider context (DCSF, 2008a), all have a direct impact on your role as an EYP in supporting and extending individual children's learning and development. Examining practice that is centred on these commitments will enable you to identify priorities within the emotional and physical environment provided in your setting.

Overriding considerations for an 'enabling environment' will be framed by the setting's compliance with the statutory requirements contained in the framework. For example, you will need to examine the extent to which your setting is 'welcoming, safe and stimulating'

(DCSF, 2008a: 19). A key question for you to consider here is how you can protect 'opportunities for learning' and enable 'children's own way of thinking and exploring' within a *safe* environment (Nutbrown, 2006: 6). Therefore, when attempting to improve elements of an 'enabling environment', it is useful to consider that 'the solution of a problem – any problem – consists in discovering how to transform an existing state of affairs into a desired one that has not yet come into being' (Donaldson, 1978: 15). Such an approach will be employed in the following reflective task, as you seek to overcome challenges identified in your existing environment.

REFLECTIVE TASK

Concept map

Reflect on the above commitments for an 'enabling environment'. Then create a concept map to record your thoughts about the existing provision of the emotional and physical environment in your setting. Consider whether any current practice could be affecting the quality of the environment and note if there are any priorities to be addressed. Identify any challenges that could form barriers to tackling these priorities. Explore possible strategies you could utilise to overcome these challenges and plan improvements for these areas. Finally, note any standards that are related to your action for improving practice and how you could evidence those standards. An example of a concept map of an 'enabling environment' is provided below in Figure 5.1.

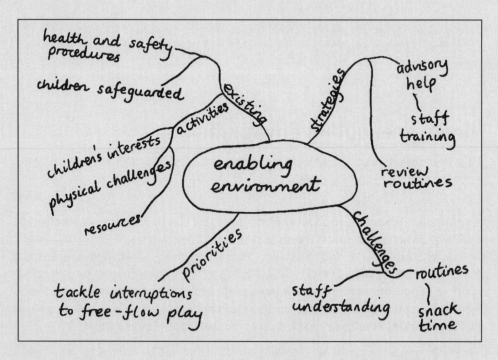

Figure 5.1 Example of a concept map of an 'enabling environment' in a private nursery

---

After creating your concept map of an 'enabling environment', you should explore how you will promote features of effective practice in your role of leading and supporting others. For example, when developing practice relating to the first commitment, consider how you could encourage practitioners in your setting to share their views about individual children, to adopt consistent and appropriate systems for observing, assessing and planning and to reflect on their practice (Fisher, 2008). You could also emphasise the importance of an outdoor learning environment that 'supports children [in] making connections, and collecting and combining their materials from a wide area' (Tovey, 2007: 75).

The environment can therefore only be considered enabling when there is due regard to the needs of the individual child. When recognising and applying features of effective practice, you can more readily select priorities whilst acknowledging the influential contextual factors relating to your setting: for example, the availability of finance, staff and other resources. Let us now consider the essential features of the learning environment, which are identified in the following checklist.

A 'learning environment' should provide:

- *a diverse, inclusive curriculum that is empowering for children and practitioners and involves parents and other adults in children's learning;*

- *new and interesting experiences that encourage self-reliance, cooperation, collaboration, responsibility and interdependence to promote children's involvement in their own learning;*

- *appropriate, content-rich and meaningful activities that foster children's natural curiosity and opportunities to investigate, question, experiment and develop competence;*

- *flexibility within the timetable that enables children to have some control over when and how experiences/activities/tasks are undertaken;*

- *adults who acknowledge, value and extend children's ways of knowing, thinking, reasoning and understanding;*

- *strategies that empower children as learners and develop their confidence;*

- *adults who will raise and respond to questions and provide challenges to extend learning;*

- *opportunities for children to engage with adults in sustained shared thinking;*

- *adults who help children to make connections between areas of learning and experience and support their independence, interdependence, choices and decisions;*

- *a range of contexts in which learning can occur – for example, outdoor areas of the setting;*

- *opportunities to play alone, in pairs and in groups;*

- *high quality, wide-ranging resources that facilitate progress, extend learning and support the development of creativity and innovation.*

(Adapted from Fisher, 2008: 81 and Wood and Attfield, 2005: 231–2)

REFLECTIVE TASK

After examining the above checklist, return to your concept map and identify any features from the checklist that are similar to those issues highlighted for development in your setting. Are there any issues on your concept map that are not featured in the checklist? Now consider how the features from the checklist apply in the following case-study.

CASE STUDY

Aislin, an EYP in a children's centre

During a review of the 'enabling environment' in her setting, Aislin, an EYP in a children's centre, identified that more opportunities should be provided for children 'to explore and learn in secure and safe, yet challenging indoor and outdoor spaces' PiP card 3.3 (DCSF, 2007c). Aislin's key concern was attitudes that were expressed by a small group of experienced practitioners. They were exhibiting 'a culture of low expectations and risk aversion' and their behaviour was leading to 'dull, unstimulating environments where the adults' focus is on containing and managing the children' (Tovey, 2007: 101). Following consultation with colleagues, Aislin drew up an action plan based on these concerns and then considered the challenges to improving practice and the options to manage these challenges:

Action plan
To raise the quality of outdoor experiences by:

- *increasing opportunities for utilising the setting's large outdoor area;*

- *arranging visits to interesting areas within the local community;*

- *encouraging practitioners to explore PiP card 3.3 (DCSF, 2007c), which highlights key issues to consider within the emotional, indoor and outdoor environment;*

- *leading sessions on observation, assessment and planning for the outdoor environment; involving multi-agency professionals in developing practitioners' understanding of safety factors; this would help to alleviate effects of the 'climate of fear' articulated by some practitioners, that can 'reduce children's autonomy' (Tovey, 2007: 100).*

Challenges to improving practice
Some staff may resist opportunities for increased use of the outdoor environment and visits to the local area and still express concerns about children's safety. Considera-tion must therefore be given to 'how it is possible to prepare practitioners for [such] change and equip them with the confidence and capabilities to meet that change' (Reed, 2008: 163).

Options to manage these challenges
Ensure that:

- *relevant staff start to experiment with the changes in practice in the outdoor environment; this should encourage them to integrate change more readily into their regular schedules within the setting (Rodd, 2006);*

- *professional development opportunities are available for staff to develop their understanding about provision of a more challenging outdoor environment;*

- *all staff are aware of the EYFS policy on outdoor play provision (DCSF, 2008b: 7);*

- *provision of an appropriate emotional environment is also considered, as 'unless learners have their physical and emotional needs met, they will be unable to learn effectively' (Wilmot, 2006: 35).*

Aislin was aware that 'having information and knowledge about parents' points of view is crucial' (Draper and Duffy, 2006: 159) when developing provision in a range of contexts, and that any parental concerns about their children's safety and other matters would need to be addressed. Aislin has already established 'effective and collaborative partnerships between local families and local professionals' (Wall, 2006: 59), which would support her engagement with parents on this issue. Following the concept of 'parents as partners' – one of the key principles of Reggio Emilia, the approach to learning that emerged in Italy after the Second World War, which recognises the 'unique reciprocal learning relationship' between adult and child (Valentine, 2006: 1) – Aislin actively promotes participation; she enables parents to suggest ideas that support children's learning and development and to offer their skills to the setting (Wood and Attfield, 2005: 129).

This case study demonstrates how the framework themes are complementary: for example, Aislin realised that a close partnership that is established between educators, parents and children is 'so important to learning' (Glauert et al., 2007: 163). You should also involve parents in decisions concerning transition arrangements affecting their children, as during periods of change 'familiar people, things, places and routines become even more important than usual' (Roberts, 2006: 135). Although Parents as Partners is a commitment contained within the theme of 'positive relationships', Aislin appreciated that different commitments may need to be integrated when considering an 'enabling environment' (DCSF, 2008a).

REFLECTIVE TASK

When you have reflected further on this case study:

- *identify standards that you think are related to Aislin's actions; then, against each of these standards, consider how your actions in your setting would meet these standards;*

- *consider Aislin's work with practitioners in her setting; how does this support her role in leading practice?*

Having explored the actions and supportive role of an EYP in leading practice, you will now need to complete the following activity, which will help you to develop an action plan centred on improving the environment in your setting. By referring to your concept map, select an area to develop and note any links to other themes/commitments you will need to consider. You should also recognise any standards that are relevant to your actions in Table 5.2

Self-assessment task

Table 5.2 Improving the environment in your setting

	Aspect of an enabling environment	Key questions	Links to EYPS
Standards			
Concerns identified in existing practice			
Action to improve practice			
Challenges to improving practice			
Influential factors (for example, finance, availability of LA support)			
Strategies to manage challenges			

You could repeat this activity with other aspects relevant to this theme or alternatively work from the starting point of another theme. Refer to the EYFS framework, including the PiP cards and CD-ROM (DCSF, 2007c; 2008d), and the recommended further reading for this section, which will assist you with the above task.

Theme 4: learning and development

Children develop and learn in different ways and at different rates and all areas of Learning and Development are equally important and inter-connected.

(DCSF, 2008a)

The commitments for Theme 4 of the EYFS are play and exploration, active learning, creativity and critical thinking and areas of learning and development (DCSF, 2008a). The first commitment is an essential consideration when you are reviewing priorities for supporting children's development and learning. The EYFS (DCSF, 2008b) stresses that children's learning is heightened during play and highlights the implications for play-based practice. All areas of learning and development 'must be delivered through planned, purposeful play, with a balance of adult-led and child-initiated activities' (DCSF, 2008a: 11).

Although play may be accepted as 'a valuable learning and developmental process' for children (Moyles, 2005: 6), you might encounter some concerns about the subject of play in settings where this activity may not be so highly valued. Fisher (2008: 132) maintains that confronting practitioners' anxieties about a play-based curriculum is an important feature of improving the quality of play in settings; otherwise the provision could be still 'highly structured and controlled by adults rather than children'.

If you experience resistance from practitioners or other adults when developing play in your setting, it could be helpful to develop a shared understanding of its value as a fundamental aspect of Early Years practice, perhaps by jointly exploring and evaluating theories of play. Tovey (2007: 19) has examined Vygotsky's (1978) belief that play leads children's development, 'as it allows children to explore meaning and contributes to the development of abstract thought'. Reflecting on play both as a process in learning and possible method of teaching is termed 'playful pedagogy' by Moyles (2005: 8). This helps us to develop more understanding about the real value of play, such as opportunities for children to use their experiences in play, and 'extend them to develop ideas, concepts and skills' (DCSF, 2007c: PiP 4.1).

When you are taking on the role of an EYP, there may be other factors to consider that could inhibit improvements to practice, for example, physical features within the setting, such as limited access to outdoor areas. Now examine possible challenges to improving play in your setting in the task below:

Explore aspects of play in your setting that could be improved and then note any challenges that may impede possible improvements. Then consider how you could overcome these challenges. Use the Table 5.3 to facilitate your reflections.

Table 5.3 Improving aspects of play

Aspects of play that could be improved	Challenges to improving play	Planned action to overcome these challenges

The above task addresses the implications for your role as an EYP, as you encourage practitioners to develop play, whilst adhering to the statutory requirements contained within the EYFS. Consistent policies regarding play must also be in place in your setting: for example, having an agreed procedure concerning practitioners' intervention, should play become 'racist, sexist or in any way offensive, unsafe, violent or bullying' (DCSF, 2007c: PiP 4.1).

As play is an intrinsic element of the EYFS framework, it is also important to consider how you will support the provision of high-quality play experiences in your setting by exploring the role of the adult during play. This is a significant feature of the Reggio Emilia approach to children's learning: for example, this approach recognises that 'talking with children, rather than to them about their work' is essential when demonstrating that adults respect their efforts (Valentine, 2006). Discussion about children's work is also one of the recommendations to develop staff practice included in Ofsted's (2007: 5) survey of 144 settings, which proposed that staff should provide 'regular, planned opportunities, including imaginative play, for children to develop their creativity and adults should discuss with them what they are doing'.

The relationship between adults and children is explored by Langston and Abbott (2007: 5), who suggest that if an adult knows a child well, 'they are "tuned" in to the child's feelings and emotions; they are both able to accept the child's feelings', even when they are powerfully expressed. This view is also expressed in the earlier work of Bruce (2004: 96), who considered that adults need to 'tune into what the child is trying to say, or is saying without words'; this process enables them to understand how the child feels and what they are thinking.

REFLECTIVE TASK

Consider how you could encourage and enable practitioners to 'tune into' children's feelings and thinking. As you explore this issue, address the following questions in turn about the practitioner's involvement in play:

- *when could they be involved?*

- *how could they be involved?*

(Adapted from Wood and Attfield, 2005: 173)

Refer to Sections 1.21 and 1.22 of the *Practice Guidance for the Early Years Foundation Stage* (DCSF, 2008b: 7–8) for suggestions on how the adult can support children's learning through play. One of the factors that you should consider when supporting practitioners is to enable them to realise 'when they should be actively involved, when to model skills and when to sit back and act as a secure base' (Manning-Morton and Thorp, 2006: 15). Note any priorities for practice that you identified and any relevant EYPS Standards.

PiP card 4.2 'Active Learning' (DCSF, 2007c), helps us to appreciate that children 'learn best through physical and mental challenges'. Practitioners can support children's involvement by challenging and extending their thinking, as they engage with objects, ideas, events, people and materials that enable them to try and solve problems.

The importance of providing 'well-planned experiences based on children's spontaneous play, both indoors and outdoors' is emphasised in the EYFS (DCSF, 2008b: 7). The implications here for effective practice are that practitioners will:

- provide opportunities for all types of play;

- present new, vibrant, first-hand experiences;

- place tasks in meaningful situations by relating them to what they are familiar with;

- introduce similar ideas in a variety of meaningful contexts;

- arrange tasks to encourage mental activity; incorporate problem-solving and investigational approaches;

- provide opportunities for self-expression;

- provide opportunities for meaningful conversations between groups of children and between children and adults. (Adapted from Whitebread, 2003: 17)

REFLECTIVE TASK

Consider the above list and reflect on the challenges and opportunities for active learning in your setting, including the provision of personalised learning. Note how your setting acknowledges that children learn and develop in various ways. How are differences in ways of learning acknowledged in planning documents?

One recent challenge for the Early Years sector is to ensure that the quality of provision is maintained alongside an increase in quantity (Pugh, 2006). However, developing a shared understanding of 'what constitutes quality' in multi-professional teams working in Early Years settings could present a further challenge, as members of a team, representing different disciplines, may employ different criteria when engaged in self-evaluation processes (Anning and Edwards, 2006: 161).

Some of the key research studies identified earlier, such as *The Effective Provision of Pre-school Education (EPPE)* (Sylva et al., 2004) and *Researching Effective Pedagogy in the Early Years (REPEY)* (Siraj-Blatchford et al., 2002) will offer you valuable insights when considering factors that affect the quality of provision. These studies identify that positive, cognitive outcomes in the most effective settings 'were associated with adult-child interactions that involve *sustained shared thinking*' (Wood and Attfield, 2005: 106). Further references to the notion of sustained shared thinking can be found in the EYFS (DCSF, 2008b: 9) and on PiP card 4.3, 'Creativity and Critical Thinking' (DCSF, 2007c). These both highlight the adult's role in developing children's understanding and extending their thinking. Ofsted (2007: 11) also underlines the importance of making links across the areas of learning; you should, therefore, consider how you can encourage children to make connections in their learning.

REFLECTIVE TASK

Reflect on an example of an interaction with a child that you consider would provide strong evidence for S16, 'Engage in sustained shared thinking with children' (CWDC: 2007a). How did you promote 'sustained, shared thinking?' Then consider how you will encourage practitioners to support children's learning by:

- *asking them open questions;*

- *working with them to develop an idea or skill;*

- *supporting and extending their thinking;*

- *enabling them to make connections.*

(Adapted from PiP card 4.3, DCSF, 2007c)

The fourth commitment (DCSF, 2008a) concerns the six areas of learning and development. The EFYS framework emphasises the connections between all six areas and underlines their equal significance. The Practice Guidance for the EYFS (DCSF, 2008b: 6) notes that practitioners 'must promote positive attitudes to diversity and difference within all children' and 'deliver personalised learning, development and care' to help children obtain the 'best possible start in life'. There are also three key elements that you need to consider relating to implementing the EYFS requirements in this area: these are the early learning goals, the educational programmes and the assessment arrangements (DfES, 2007a). An important aspect of your role as an EYP will therefore be to plan effectively, incorporating an appreciation for children's individual interests and abilities, to enhance their learning and development (DCSF, 2007c: PiP 4.4).

Postscript

The *Children's Plan: Building Brighter Futures* (DCSF, 2007b) emphasises the significance of the EYFS framework in enabling better outcomes for children. The framework takes a dynamic and responsive approach and you will need to be aware of any supplementary practice guidance that will inform your role as an EYP.

C H A P T E R   S U M M A R Y

In this chapter we have focused on meeting the challenges of implementing the EYFS. The four themes of the framework have provided the structure for exploring key issues that you will need to examine when leading and supporting others. You have considered opportunities for meeting standards for EYPS and reflected on your role as an agent of change when leading practice across the EYFS.

Moving on

In the next chapter, we explore some aspects of teamwork and discuss how the EYP can meet the challenges of leading practice within a team context. In particular, we focus on some of the essential skills required by the EYP in leading practice effectively within a team setting.

Elfer, P., Goldschmied, E. and Selleck, D. (2003) *Key Persons in the Nursery: Building Relationships for Quality Provision*. London: David Fulton.

Fisher, J. (2008) *Starting from the Child: Teaching and Learning in the Foundation Stage* (3rd edn). Maidenhead: Open University Press (Chapters 5 and 7).

6 Leadership of collaborative practice and teamwork

CHAPTER OBJECTIVES

In this chapter we explore how the EYP can meet the challenges of leading practice within a team context, though acknowledge that this is NOT the same as the 'team leader' role. We identify the importance of emotional and social intelligence in leading practice effectively within a team and the essential interpersonal and communication skills for this aspect of practice are outlined. The importance of understanding roles within teams are highlighted and factors that contribute to team success are discussed with reference to theories and models that can aid understanding of the behaviour of staff, within different work contexts. Through case study examples and reflective activities, you will have the opportunity to discern the importance of your role as a supportive leader of change, who values each team member.

After reading this chapter you should be able to:
- discuss factors that contribute to effective teamwork;
- reflect critically on the importance of social and emotional intelligence and strong interpersonal skills in leading practice within a team;
- appraise critically your own strengths and areas for development in this area;
- apply your understanding to the preparation of your evidence for EYP validation.

This chapter focuses specifically on EYP Standards 33–35 but you are encouraged to reflect broadly across the other Standards as you seek to apply your knowledge, understanding and skills in teamwork to all aspects of your practice.

Introduction

You will be able to draw experiences of some of the positive and negative aspects of teamwork. In leading the Early Years Foundation Stage (EYFS), very few of you will work in isolation and the intention in this chapter is that you should focus on the 'collaborative' aspect of your role, even if you work in an isolated context most of the time. Most of you will be part of a team of colleagues and/or other professionals, all working together towards a common goal or outcome, that of providing the highest possible quality provision and practice for young children across the EYFS.

We will consider briefly some of the relevant theoretical frameworks that apply to building effective teams and focus on the skills and attributes required by the EYP in leading practice in a team context, even when not in the explicit role of 'team leader'. We look, however, not just at the *formation* of strong teams but how these can be *maintained* over a period of time. Sometimes things go wrong in teams and we explore how the EYP might be alert to early indicators of difficulties and how s/he can support stronger relationships between team members, even in conflict situations.

Teams

What is a 'team'? Dictionary definitions all offer some variation of 'a number of persons associated in some joint action'. This is quite different from a 'group' which is simply a collection of individuals who happen to be in the same place at the same time but not necessarily bound by any common purpose. Duck (2001) suggests that teamwork is essentially about working together for the common good, being committed to the same goals and helping each other to achieve these. He goes on to say that 'failure to create that kind of teamwork can be fatal to the entire change effort' (Duck, 2001: 95)

Rodd's early research (1998) in England and Australia adds a further dimension to the definition of a team when applied to early childhood settings. She found the element of cooperation between team members to be significant, with the achievement of an agreed set of aims or goals balanced with 'consideration of the personal needs and interests of individuals within the team' (Rodd, 1998: 100).

Rosie, a room leader in the full-day care provision of a children's centre, Toni, a supervisor of a voluntary pre-school, and Rahana, a registered childminder, describe their different experiences of being part of team:

CASE STUDY

Rosie

'Each week all the room leaders meet with the manager for briefing and review. I make sure our room team meets prior to this and provide opportunity for colleagues to share any concerns or issues they wish me to take to the manager's briefing. At the meeting, the manager always encourages each of us to share our views and ideas. We each feel really valued by him and know he appreciates the way we share leadership with him.'

CASE STUDY

Toni

'I have always been a highly energetic person with lots of drive and thought I was a good team leader. Our recent Ofsted inspection highlighted the strong leadership in the pre-school. However, I overheard one of my staff saying that I didn't give them enough opportunity to make decisions but really just expected them to rubber-stamp my ideas. I didn't say anything immediately but reflected on this later and recognised my own reluctance to delegate. I questioned my own practice: did I not trust my staff's judgements?'

89

Rahana

'It is not easy for me to think immediately in terms of working in a team but then I remember that each week, I take my minded children to the local childminders' network play session at the community centre. There we each take turns to lead the song and story session for all the children and usually discuss together different aspects of our practice. Last week, Sara wanted to know about my experiences with Salid, one of my minded children, who is two and a half and who is very inquisitive with lots of "why?" and "how?" questions, and some of the activities I plan for him. Sara has a new little girl starting with her who is a lot like that, too.'

REFLECTIVE TASK

- *What are the differences between these three teams in the case studies?*

- *In terms of team effectiveness, how critical is the way the leaders see their role?*

- *Can you see how Rosie, Toni and Rahana might use these reflections to support their evidence for S33, and for other Standards?*

Team formation

You may well be familiar with Tuckman's (1965) seminal work on team formation based on the fundamental principles that teams, like all other living organisms, go through different stages of development and are not static. The original Tuckman model had four linear stages, though Tuckman with Jensen (1977) later added a fifth. In reality, it is unlikely that these stages are as sequential as thus presented, and some teams will seem to spend longer in one stage and even miss one out altogether. However, it remains a useful model in helping us to understand team processes and Table 6.1 is an adaptation of Tuckman and Jensen's model where the dimension and challenges of leadership are considered (Isaksen and Tidd, 2006). Look at this and then complete the reflective task.

REFLECTIVE TASK

Think of an opportunity you have had to work with a team on a project or innovation. Are you aware of the stages the team went through in this task? Reflect particularly on your experience of leading the beginning ('forming') and ending ('transforming') stages in this.

Table 6.1 Stages of team development

Stage	Characterised by	Leadership dimensions
1. FORMING (orientation towards team identity)	Uncertainty and anxiety about other team members and the tasks/goals	Possible over-dependence on you. Important to clarify the tasks, provide the structures and encourage confidence
2. STORMING	Interpersonal tension: possible conflict between team members – may be overt or covert	Facilitative leadership is required which acknowledges diversity and models effective and sensitive listening each to the other
3. NORMING	A sense of 'belongingness' is established with conflict resolved	Importance of leader recognising the group's success and rewarding this appropriately
4. PERFORMING	A growing sense of inter-dependence among team members and cooperation in task achievement; some risk-taking	Key leadership task is to keep the team on track but also allow them scope and autonomy in 'performance'
5. TRANSFORMING (sometimes also called ADJOURNING)	Task completed/goal achieved; celebration of success and of positive relationships formed mixed reactions to 'ending' of team or task	If team disbands, leader's role is to reflect on success and what can be learned from it and to provide appropriate 'ending'; if team is to continue on to new task, there may be new members to include and new goals to negotiate

Team-building

The successful functioning of any team is dependent on each individual member functioning well, where each person acts as a kind of catalyst to the other. As we discussed in the previous chapter, EYP Standard 33 requires you to 'establish and sustain a culture of collaborative and cooperative working between colleagues' (CWDC, 2007a: 9) There are two elements here: the establishment of *building* of a team and then its *maintenance*.

Edgington (2004) suggests that there are three main types of team in Early Years settings:

- **the cosy team:** usually well-established; members have worked together for a long time; systems and organisation works well for them; show a united hostility to new ways of working; not welcoming to new members; attitude to change is to ignore it;

- **the turbulent team:** on the surface all appears to be well; at meetings the majority accept the decisions of the few; but outside, strong disagreement/disquiet may be expressed behind the backs of those most vocal at meetings; change is difficult to effect because there is no clear dialogue for shared decision-making;

- **the rigorous and challenging team:** professional approach; outward looking with a strong commitment to continuing professional development; regular reviews of practice; do not always agree but will discuss issues critically and try to reach a consensus ; open to change but with a thoughtful, well-prepared approach; never fully satisfied with what they are doing and challenge each other.

REFLECTIVE TASK

- *Have you any experience of working in any such teams?*
- *Reflect on the positives and negatives of this experience.*
- *If you have experience of two types, what were the main differences in effectiveness?*
- *What are the particular challenges for the leader in each type of team?*

There is a plethora of literature devoted to team-building (Dyer, 1987; Williams, 1996; West, 2004) which is a clear indicator of its importance to organisational success. There are two main dimensions involved in team-building: staff morale and task demands (Rodd, 2006). The role of the leader is to hold these two in tension, recognising that a task will not be achieved if members of staff feel uncertain of what is involved, are lacking in confidence or feeling under-valued. However, equally, the leader needs to hold fast to the achievement of the goal that has been identified and not be deflected from the task. Gillen (1995, cited in Smith and Langston, 1999: 44) describes four principles in the process of building a team:

- **pull, don't push** – allow the team, not the leader, to set the pace;

- **involve people as much as possible** – encourage the team to think through ideas and take ownership of them;

- **think behaviour rather than personality** – observe individual behaviours rather than labelling their actions;

- **persuade, don't manipulate** – respect the other person and try to see their point of view.

As an EYP, it is important that you apply some of these principles to your role as leader of practice. The work of Neugabauer and Neugabauer (1998, cited in Rodd, 2006: 163–4) is significant here. They offer a five-step framework for team-building in early childhood settings:

- **set achievable goals** – mutually agreed by all team members;

- **clarify and explain roles** – where individual roles are clear to all and free of conflict; the leader's role in identifying all the tasks required and individuals to undertake these is key here;

- **build supportive relationships** – developing trust (see Chapter 5) and providing resources to develop a cooperative team spirit;

- **encourage active participation** – capitalise on the skills and knowledge of each team member;

- **monitor team effectiveness** – build in regular opportunities to assess goal achievement and teamworking.

Look at the following case study and consider how Cali, the baby room leader within a children's centre, might apply insights from theory to building the team in her room.

CASE STUDY

Cali has only been in this setting for two months. She has recently learned that one of the other practitioners in the baby room also applied for the post of leader but Cali – an external applicant – was appointed. Cali feels that the current organisation of the baby room places too much emphasis on the babies' care needs with little priority given to providing stimulating and developmentally appropriate learning activities for them. There is direct access to a small outdoor area from the room but current practice does not include regular use of this.

REFLECTIVE TASK

How might Cali apply the five-step approach (Neugabauer and Neugabauer, 1998) in her leadership role?

Group dynamics and roles within teams

The work of Meredith Belbin (1993) has been hugely significant in helping us understand the different roles required for effective teamwork. Table 6.2 is a summary of these: you can access further details at http://www.belbin.com/downloads/Belbin_Team_Role_Summary_Descriptions.pdf.

It is worth taking a moment to reflect that one of the roles of the leader of practice is to understand the individuality of each team member and to embrace diversity. The principles highlighted earlier relating to equality practice with children and families apply equally to working with a diverse team of colleagues. While Belbin's roles fit more naturally into the business arena, they are useful in helping you to see the complementary nature of the different roles within a team – where diversity is viewed as an opportunity and not as a threat. Belbin's notion that with each team strength comes 'allowable weaknesses' is a very important one for the leader to apply to practice.

Table 6.2 Belbin's team roles

Team role	Contribution to teamwork	Allowable weakness
PLANT	Creative problem-solver	Can be over-focused and fail to communicate effectively
RESOURCE INVESTIGATOR	Enthusiastic explorer of opportunities; develops contacts/networks	Can be over-optimistic and lose interest when obstacles appear
COORDINATOR	Mature; confident; delegates; promotes decision making	May be seen as manipulative
SHAPER	Challenging; dynamic; thrives on pressure; can overcome obstacles	Often hurts people's feelings; makes unthinking remarks
MONITOR EVALUATOR	Strategic and discerning; grasps overview of a situation and judges accurately	Lacks dynamism and the ability to inspire others
TEAM WORKER	Cooperative; listens; gets on with task; averts friction	Indecisive at crunch points
IMPLEMENTER	Disciplined; reliable and efficient; turns ideas into practice	Often inflexible and slow to respond to new ideas
COMPLETER FINISHER	Painstaking; conscientious; reliable; thorough	Inclined to worry unduly and reluctant to delegate
SPECIALIST	Single-minded; dedicated; provides specialist skills/knowledge	Makes contribution only on narrow front

---

REFLECTIVE TASK

Look again at the list of team roles, contributions to teamwork and their allowable weaknesses.

- *Do you recognise your own personal role in your team context?*

- *Can you identify others in your team who assume some of the other roles?*

- *What are the particular challenges for the EYP in leading practice within a team where each member brings both positive contributions and allowable weaknesses?*

As an EYP, you also need to take account of the dynamics within your team. These are generally defined as interactions between team members in such a manner that each person influences and is influenced by each other person (Shaw, 1976). The impact of positive dynamics is team cohesion, whereas when negative factors are in play these can undermine team effectiveness. The following 'S' factors can affect cohesion.

- **stability** – the longer the team is together with the same members, the greater the opportunity for cohesion;

- **similarity** – the more similar the team members are in terms of age, gender, skills and attitudes, the greater the cohesion;

- **size** – the larger the group, the more challenging cohesion becomes;

- **support** – the more effectively teams are led and managed, the greater the cohesion;

- **satisfaction** – cohesion is associated with the extent to which team members are pleased with each others' performance, behaviour and commitment to the common task.

(McCauley et al., 1998)

Consider the following two scenarios in two separate Early Years settings.

Setting 1: Jingles Nursery is a popular private provider of Early Years provision for children from three months to five years. Jo, the owner manager, has had overall responsibility for the nursery since it was established ten years ago and has built up strong rapport with her staff and with the families who use the nursery. There are 12 staff members altogether, half of whom have also been employed there since it opened. All members of staff are women and all have comparable Early Years qualifications, except for Suzi who joined the staff six months ago and who has a degree in childhood studies. Jo deals with all the day-to-day running of the nursery and there are prescriptive systems in place for planning, monitoring and reporting children's progress. There are three room leaders, one of whom is Suzi, and all are committed to high quality practice. Suzi has recently decided to proceed to validation for EYPS.

Setting 2: Jangles Pre-School is a voluntary setting catering for the needs of children from two to five years. Jak is the new playleader and a number of staff have moved on since she arrived a year ago. Jak has found it hard to recruit qualified practitioners to replace those who have left and two new staff members tend to have very different ideas from Jak about practice while another lacks confidence and is very dependent on Jak for support and guidance.

REFLECTIVE TASK

- *What factors affect cohesion at Jingles Nursery? What are the particular leadership challenges faced by Jo and Suzi?*

- *What factors affect cohesion at Jangles Pre-School? What are the particular challenges facing Jak and the whole staff team there?*

Team effectiveness

The characteristics of an effective team can be summarised by a sense of common purpose and clear objectives; a workable balance of roles within the team; a shared and (mainly) equal commitment from all team members; and effective communication and dialogue within the team (Daly et al., 2004).

Clearly, an effective team is one where there is a high degree of satisfaction because the targets it sets itself are achieved. Rodd's (1998) research on the factors that contribute to job satisfaction within Early Years teams offers valuable insights here. As you read the list, you might like to think about your role in leading practice and your own contribution to team effectiveness:

- support and stimulation;

- a sense of belonging and equality;

- opportunity for growth and development;

- stress reduction;

- facilitation of a pleasant working environment;

- opportunity to work through issues and the minimalisation of conflict;

- the opportunity to role-model team effectiveness to children and families;

- the opportunities for all team members to take a lead role on some aspect of practice and provision;

- shared work load and mutual encouragement in the achievement of the common task;

- shared human resources, ideas and skills;

- acknowledgement of each member's professional capabilities.

One of your tasks as EYP is to maximise team effectiveness and identify and minimise any hindering factors that prevent successful teamwork, especially in leading the EYFS and in implementing change. Even where you are not officially in the role of team leader, within your responsibilities as a leader of practice it is important that you are able to analyse and evaluate the strengths and weaknesses of the team with whom you are working and seeking to lead. Isaksen and Tidd (2006: 185) refer to the 'assets and liabilities' of any team, which concurs with Belbin's work on the positive contributions and allowable weakness of each team member. The potential 'liabilities' and difficulties in teamwork are considered in the final section of this chapter but here we consider the potential strengths of teamwork, which include the following:

- greater availability of knowledge and information;

- more opportunity for shared thinking, thus increasing the likelihood of building and developing the ideas of others;

- a wide range of experiences, perspectives and (human) resources on which to draw;

- increased understanding and ownership of team outcomes drawn from participation and involvement in decision-making and problem-solving;

- opportunities for personal and professional development through increasing team cohesion, communication and companionship.

REFLECTIVE TASK

Think of opportunities you have in your current role in leading practice to nurture cohesion, communication and companionship between colleagues.

- *How might you model these aspects of teamwork more effectively?*

- *What impact do you believe effective teamwork has on the children's experiences?*

- *Can you link your reflection here to S33?*

We cannot leave discussion on team effectiveness without reflecting briefly on the variables identified by Burton and Dimbleby (1988) which can affect teams. These are person variables, environmental variables and task variables. Holding together the different abilities – and for the EYP this can often be expressed in the different levels of experience and training of the Early Years practitioners (Siraj-Batchford et al., 2002) – personality traits, motives and value stances of individual team members requires skilled leadership. Person variables may also include staff changes and the challenges of recruitment. The environmental variables include specific factors relating to the immediate setting, to available resources, wider issues in the community and indeed to national policy. The tasks and aspects of practice being addressed will vary also but for the EYP will focus on quality delivery of EYFS provision, and the skilled EYP will recognise that different team members will approach the variety of tasks in distinctive ways. Human resource management is clearly an important component of the role of leader of practice!

Bill is deputy manager of a workplace nursery, funded by the company for its personnel. Bill's role includes that of lead practitioner with the three–five-year-olds but the manager is on long-term sick leave so Bill is having to spend more time out of direct contact with the children and practice. He has delegated responsibility for day-to-day leadership of practice in the pre-school room to Siobhan, who is very anxious about this and continually wants to 'talk things over' with Bill. A current development project in the nursery is the installation of new wooden furniture across all base rooms. One morning, Bill receives a phone call from a distressed parent of one of the babies expressing concern that after collecting her baby the evening before, she had found a bruise on her baby's leg which looked like the imprint of adult fingerprints.

Think of the person, environmental and task variables which Bill (and others in the staff team) face at the present time. What effect might these be having on team cohesion and effectiveness? What leadership skills will Bill need to apply in dealing with these current challenges?

Leadership of practice with a team

As we have stressed, the role of EYP is not to be confused with that of team leader, but we have identified that leadership of practice is usually carried out in a team context and in this section, we focus specifically on different aspects of the EYP role as leader within a team. Becoming an effective team requires the commitment and effort of every team member but in leading practice, particularly in effecting change, you may well have a crucial role in determining team cohesion.

The EYP should demonstrate principled leadership (Isaksen and Tidd, 2006; Rodd, 2006). We have already identified the importance of the value stance of the leader of practice, leading by example, encouraging and implementing new ideas and sharing best practices. The principled leader recognises that some in the team will need more support than others, requiring encouragement to express their own ideas confidently within the team. The model of leadership demonstrated by the EYP is not one that exerts authority over others but rather one that empowers each individual to maximise her/his distinctive contribution to the whole. This is collaborative leadership: Whalley (2005b) refers to such a dynamic as a 'leaderful team' where all are committed to 'growing learning communities'.

One of your key tasks as leader of practice, then, is to engage all relevant members of your team in identifying the challenges and opportunities for improvements in your setting and then sharing responsibility for transforming ideas into action. Pound (2005) refers to this as 'distributed leadership' and this is useful in enhancing our understanding of the EYP leadership role, especially in effecting change. You will need to demonstrate competence in taking a lead in collaborative decision-making.

Look at these examples from three EYPs, showing how they have evidenced S33–35.

Example 1 – Kate, proprietor and manager of a day nursery:

'I worked with each of the heads of room in the setting and together we modelled to the rest of the team how to note down daily observations of activities that the children had particularly enjoyed, particular achievements etc. and then to reflect on how this learning might be extended. I then encouraged each team to use these observations to inform the following week's plans.'

Example 2 – Angela, advisory teacher for a group of private nurseries:

'Working across different settings has been particularly challenging but I spent a lot of time building up good relationships with individual managers and colleagues in our settings and aimed to model to them the importance of close teamwork, with each making their own personal contribution to the setting. Together we discussed the Ofsted inspection framework and how our practice should aim to incorporate the *Every Child Matters* outcomes into everyday practice. I produced a 'Care, Learning and Inclusion' file for each setting and worked with staff on a monitoring sheet which is used to regularly appraise how this is going.'

Example 3 – Joanne, manager of a private nursery:

'I know I still have a lot to learn and am prepared to develop my skills continually. I believe communication is very positive in the nursery and my staff have a lot of respect for me and I value this. I know the staff appreciate the support I give them in the rooms and are always proud to share with me their ideas and achievements. I take time to listen to their ideas and tease them out so that decisions about changes to practice are shared'

Example 4 – Lewis, co-supervisor in a pre-school:

'I was an accountant before I made a career change to Early Years practice and never considered myself to have 'leadership skills'. I really like the fact that Sonia (co-leader) and I share responsibilities here but even then we would rarely impose our ideas on the team. Instead, we review practice at our monthly team meetings and when we have a particular challenge or opportunity, such as the water-logged outdoor play area we have at present, we all brainstorm possible solutions and share action on these.'

REFLECTIVE TASK

- *How are Kate, Angela, Joanne and Lewis each demonstrating a collaborative leadership style?*

- *Can you begin to identify examples from your practice which demonstrate your own skill here and you might use as evidence as you prepare for EYP validation?*

Interpersonal skills in leadership of practice

Communication and interpersonal skills are identified explicitly and implicitly in the EYP Standards: with children (S26); parents and families (S30); colleagues (S34); and other professionals (S36). We identified the importance of an assertive communication approach to the EYP role in Chapter 5 but here we focus on interpersonal skills, particularly with colleagues. Rodd (2006) believes that successful leadership in early childhood is essentially about clear communication.

Effective communication and interpersonal relationships are the building blocks for successful EYFS provision and for innovative practice generally. We have already identified that team members need to have unequivocal trust and confidence in the leader and this must stem from the leader's own self-assurance and self-esteem. For the leader in early childhood, Rodd (2006) identifies five key elements to effective communication and we consider these here in the context of the EYP role.

First, the leader needs to send clear, accurate and unambiguous messages to the team. Of course, this is equally true of communication with the children, parents and other professionals. However, sometimes the practitioner who is skilled at speaking and listening to children and encouraging their language development is not always so skilled in communicating with colleagues. As well as an assertive, calm but warm tone, it is important to think about the following:

- **what** you have to convey;
- **to whom** you are conveying the message/information;
- **how** you will convey the message/information.

The 'how' will need to be adapted to fit the 'what' and 'to whom' here. For instance, conveying news to a room leader about a windfall of £500 to spend on outdoor resources requires rather a different approach from sharing concerns with a new member of staff about her missed opportunities to note down observations of her key children.

Second, it is important to identify and overcome any existing and potential barriers to effective communication. This can be very challenging in settings that open 52 weeks a year from 7.30am to 6pm (or even later) and where there is a large staff team, with a shift system operating and a combination of full- and part-time staff. The skilled leader will try to eliminate or at least minimise such barriers. Written communication, though time-consuming for the leader, is one solution and, certainly, offers one clear solution to such challenges. Written guidance is particularly important when leading changes to practice – especially if it can include a summative account of everyone's contribution to new ideas and decision-making and an unambiguously stated action plan.

However, such barriers to effective communication are not always physical and EYPs need to be equally alert to possible psychological barriers that might exist. This is where the message or information becomes skewed because of the underlying value stance or belief of the listener. This is usually based on attitudes – often unconscious – that are prejudiced and unthinking and the skilled leader should 'not underestimate the power of psychological barriers to interpersonal interactions' (Rodd, 2006: 74). Jasmine, EYP in a private nursery, describes her experience here.

Jasmine

'I had been in the setting for a number of months and thought I was building up strong rapport with most of the team. One of the aspects I was particularly concerned about was the way that creative activities were planned and organised for the children – especially the over twos. Historically, staff would set out a limited amount of resources and have a sample of the "finished product" to show to children. Some of the staff had likewise shared their concerns about this so we worked together to implement a much more child-initiated approach where the children were free to choose their own resources, work at their own pace and produce – or not! – their own "end products". We shared this at our staff meeting. Sylvia was one of the practitioners in the setting who was still rather wary of me and my role but I was not prepared for her reaction to these changes. She did not come to me directly but spoke to the room leader saying that she would have nothing to do with this approach, the parents wanted to see "proper art work" and this approach was going to create a lot of "unnecessary mess" in the base room.'

REFLECTIVE TASK

Think about this scenario from the perspectives of both Jasmine and Sylvia.

- *Can you suggest ways that Jasmine might work with Sylvia from this point to address the psychological barrier that exists here?*

- *What opportunities for effective leadership of practice does such a situation offer?*

The third component for the leader to consider in communicating effectively is active listening. It appears that people speak at around 100–175 words per minute but have the capacity to listen intelligently to up to 300 words per minute (Fowler, 2005). However, it is all too easy to go into 'mind drift', becoming distracted and thinking about other things while appearing to listen. In fact, hearing is a biological process, where sound is transmitted from one source and received by another, but listening is a total communication process involving cognitive and emotional skills. This is why active listening is so important. This is listening with a purpose: it may be to gain information, understand another's viewpoint, work on a shared problem, identify another's feeling or show support. In the EYP role, it is important that you develop active listening skills, ensuring that sufficient time and space are allowed for the speaker and using effective eye contact and non-verbal indicators to show genuine interest in what is being said. As part of your leadership role, you should show that you want to know more, and particularly to understand what the speaker might be feeling. You should also check that you have heard accurately and ask for further clarification if necessary. Active listening results in the speaker feeling that what has been shared has been heard and taken very seriously. This process communicates the unconditional respect of the listener for the speaker and encourages further communication and interaction.

Of course, active listening will require an appropriate response and this is the fourth element in effective communication that Rodd identifies. Here, she draws on the earlier work of Carl Rogers (1961), who delineates five different response types that can be used to follow active listening. Rogers suggests that individuals may have a preferred type out of these but that each will be appropriately supported by what we call 'encouragers': the nods/shakes of the head, grunts, groans and grimaces we use to support our words. Look at Rogers' five response types in Table 6.3, and some of the ways these might be expressed.

Table 6.3 The five response types

Advising and evaluating	'What you should do now is. . .' 'If I were you, I would . . .'
Interpreting and analysing	'The problem you really have here is . . .' 'I think that is where you went wrong . . .'
Supporting and placating	'Don't worry, we all go through this . . .'
Questioning and probing	'When did you first begin to feel this . . .?' 'Have there been other times when you've experienced this. . .?'
Understanding or reflecting	'Clearly, you're concerned about the impact on the staff team to this change in the way snack time is organised.'

REFLECTIVE TASK

Effective leaders in early childhood contexts will be aware of the advantages and limitations of the different response types and . . . determine the most productive for meeting others' needs in the situation.

(Rodd, 2006:77)

- *How does the leader determine the appropriate type of response?*

- *Can you think of examples when you have used any/all of Rogers' (1961) response types in different situations within your leadership role?*

- *Do you agree with Rogers that the 'understanding or reflecting' response is that which is most under-used and under-developed by professionals? Why do you think this is?*

The fifth element in effective communication is that of the leader managing her/his own feelings appropriately. The EYP is only human! You will often have a demanding task, balancing the – sometimes unrealistic – expectations, challenges and needs of children, staff, parents and yourself. Such situations can and frequently do result in strong emotional reactions. It is important to be sufficiently self-aware to recognise such personal reactions and feelings and occasional self-disclosure can be helpful. But it is equally – if not more – essential that you maintain a professional and emotionally intelligent manner which does not undermine the confidence and trust of your colleagues.

In the final chapter of the book, we turn our attention to the EYP role of identifying and managing her/his own programme of continuing professional development (CPD) and leading others to develop their own skills and competences. But before we leave our current focus on leading practice with a team, it is important to note here McCauley et al.'s (1998) suggestion that one of the main arena for leadership development is through team development. Within a team, there is limitless opportunity for self-awareness and personal reflection and this is almost always informed through the critical lens of colleagues (Brookfield, 1995). Individual learning and organisational or practice development are 'bound to meet' (McCauley et al., 1998: 423) Your role as leader is not a static or 'finished' one but is constantly evolving and adapting to all the variables in your particular context.

Managing conflict situations in teams

In order to lead practice effectively, the EYP requires social skills and emotional intelligence. Much has been documented about 'emotional intelligence' (see, for example, Gardner, 1983; Goleman, 1996). Increasingly, emotional factors have become a recognised aspect of educational thinking and practice (Moyles, 2001). Recently, this focus was translated into policy when children's social and emotional well-being was highlighted as an essential concern for all organisations that work with children in the Government's publication of *Every Child Matters* (DfES, 2004a). The emotional dimension is, therefore, currently pertinent to your role as an EYP. This awareness of emotional matters has been conceptualised as 'emotional literacy' (Bubb, 2005).

Such emotional intelligence is critical to managing difficulties that can arise within teams. Few people welcome conflict but a healthy and emotionally intelligent attitude recognises that it is an inevitable part of teamwork and, indeed, the process of conflict resolution can often result in a stronger team (Noone, 1996). Within the EYP role, you should recognise the importance of modelling an appropriate way to deal with conflict situations constructively and creatively,

Conflict can be caused by the following:

- mis- or incomplete information;
- resistance to change;
- pressure to conform – limiting individual preferences;
- 'group think' – where the group converges on a decision that seems to have greatest agreement regardless of quality;

- dominant individuals and the consequent inequality of influence on decisions and outcomes;

- inability to accept feedback or criticism;

- lack of individual accountability – 'the team takes ownership';

- interpersonal conflict – unproductive levels of competition leading to 'winners' and 'losers'. (Based on Isaksen and Tidd, 2005).

In identifying and addressing any of these challenges to effective teamwork, the skilled EYP should employ conflict resolution strategies, including active listening; observing and noting any non-verbal clues; helping those involved to understand and define the problem; allowing feelings to be expressed; looking for alternative, workable solutions; and encouraging individuals involved to take responsibility to implement these solutions (Armstrong, 1994, cited in Rodd, 2006).

CASE STUDY

Vic

Vic is room leader of the pre-school group in an independent nursery. He works very well with two other colleagues, Betty (who has worked in the nursery for 20 years) and Judith. When Judith begins her maternity leave, Tammy joins the team to cover for her. Tammy has only recently qualified as an Early Years practitioner and is confident and enthusiastic, with lots of ideas about how Early Years practice should be organised. Vic and Tammy establish a strong rapport but Vic soon begins to notice the change in Betty who becomes quite withdrawn, arrives at the last minute and leaves as soon as she can at the end of day, contributes little in team meetings, and generally appears to be losing her enthusiasm for her work. Vic realises this is having an impact on team morale and indirectly on the quality of provision for the children.

REFLECTIVE TASK

- *What do you think is happening in this scenario?*

- *What leadership skills will Vic need to manage this situation effectively?*

- *Can you identify similar scenarios from your own practice, and if so, what was your role in resolving these?*

C   H   A   P   T   E   R   S   U   M   M   A   R   Y

Through reading this chapter, we hope you will feel clearer about the kind of evidence you might find to meet S33–36. We have reflected on how Tuckman's (1965) theory of team formation and Belbin's (1993) theory of team roles can help us understand more about the teams in which we work. In reflecting on the role of the EYP in leading practice within a team, we have identified the importance of a principled and collaborative approach, effective communication and interpersonal skills and the need for the EYP to be emotionally literate. The strengths and opportunities of teamwork have been identified along with some of the things that can go wrong in teams when the EYP will need to demonstrate skills in managing conflict.

Moving on

In the next chapter, we consider the interpersonal aspects of the EYP role further and you will have the opportunity to apply much of your thinking and learning from this chapter specifically to your role as mentor to colleagues. The concept of the mentor will be discussed and the mentor-mentee relationship explored, especially in the way it can promote successful practice and effect change.

Self-assessment questions

Use this exercise to reflect on your learning from this chapter and to think further about your skills in leading practice within a team context.

1. Think again about Tuckman and Jensen's work on the five stages on team formation. Focus on the performing stage and think about how teams reach the point of 'optimum performance' (Answer: page 91). How does the EYP lead practice in such a way as to maximise the potential of each team member?

2. What is distinctive about Belbin's (1993) work on team roles and the defining of contributions that each role brings to a team (Answer: page 94)? What have you learned about the different roles played by colleagues in your setting's team?

3. What are the five 'S' factors that can affect group/team cohesion (Answer: page 95)? Think of your setting. Are these positive or negative factors in your team's setting? What can you do about any hindering factors?

4. What are the four principles outlined by Gillen (1995) for building and maintaining an effective team (Answer: page 92)? How far do you believe you put these into practice in your own role as leader of practice?

5. What are the three types of variable in any team identified by Burton and Dimbleby (1988) (Answer: page 97)? How do you ensure you take each of these into account when you lead practice?

6. Remind yourself of Rodd's five key elements of the communication skills required by the leader of practice (Answer: pages 100–103). Prepare a table with three columns and six rows and complete as follows:

Element of communication for leadership	Reflection on practice and links to the EYP Standards	Action points

7. What are some of the possible causes of tension and conflict in a team (Answer: pages 103–104)? What skills does the EYP need in order to role-model healthy relationships and to help resolve conflict where it exists?

FURTHER READING

The Mind Tools website offers some useful guidance on the communication and interpersonal skills required by leaders. The two web pages here will direct you to useful papers on active listening and one in managing conflict situations in teams:

http://www.mindtools.com/CommSkll/Mind%20Tools%20Listening.pdf

http://www.mindtools.com/pages/article/newLDR_81.htm

7 Leading others: the role of mentoring

CHAPTER OBJECTIVES

This chapter examines the role of the Early Years Professional (EYP) in supporting and mentoring other practitioners, which is a significant and dynamic aspect of their wider remit to lead practice across the Early Years Foundation Stage (EYFS) (DCSF, 2008a).

After reading this chapter you should be able to:
- be more familiar with the EYP's mentoring role and aware of factors that impact on this role;
- identify relevant skills and attributes required to effectively undertake mentoring;
- reflect on your own performance as a mentor and examine areas for further development.

When engaged in mentoring, you will have opportunities to address how you influence and lead the practice of others with regard to several Standards for Early Years Professional Status (EYPS), particularly S33–9.

Introduction

This chapter explores the role of mentoring, a significant and dynamic aspect of your work as an EYP. You will consider how to advise, nurture and support other practitioners, enabling them to deliver services that provide better outcomes for children.

We begin by examining the role of supporting and mentoring other practitioners, building on the skills required for effective teamwork that were identified and discussed in the previous chapter. You will have the opportunity to explore skills and behaviours that support EYPs in their mentoring role and consider how these might enable you to manage and develop your own mentoring practice effectively. Throughout this section, you should also reflect on the ways in which you apply the following three skills, which are fundamental to your work as a mentor and also integral to meeting the Standards for EYPs:

- the ability to make decisions on the basis of sound judgement;

- the ability to lead and support others;

- the ability to relate to, and communicate with, others. (CWDC, 2007b: 9)

Look at Table 7.1, which maps the EYP skills to some examples of their application to mentoring. Now reflect on how your mentor has applied the EYP skills and then think about any further applications that could be included in this table.

Table 7.1 EYP skills

EYP skill (CWDC, 2007b)	Example applications
The ability to make decisions on the basis of sound judgement	– implemented a new health and safety policy and explained this to staff – involved professionals from other agencies to support a child
The ability to lead and support others	– led training on the use of ICT – worked alongside practitioners to evaluate use of the outdoor area
The ability to relate to, and communicate with, others	– devised a key worker record sheet – created an information booklet for staff to use with parents, explaining the transition process for their children

We have started to explore some skills that are involved in mentoring; these will be considered further in the following section. Then we move on to examine some factors which may impact on the mentoring process and the chapter concludes with an exploration of your own effectiveness as a mentor.

Mentoring

A community is the sum of its parts. If the development of those individual parts is full, the result will lead to what is good for the whole.

(Samaras, 2002: 147).

Several definitions of the mentoring role within the school sector can be found in the growing body of literature on the subject (Levy, 2007). From your perspective as an EYP, however, it is particularly useful to explore and establish an understanding of what it means to provide support and mentor others who work across the variety of settings that constitute Early Years provision (CWDC: 2007a). According to Rodd (2006), one of the qualities that successful mentors exhibit is an understanding of the mentor's role. You have already explored the application of the three EYP skills (CWDC, 2007b) in the reflective task above; now complete the following task to help you consider your wider interpretation of the mentoring role:

We are able to develop a better understanding of the role and how to become good mentors ourselves by first considering how we have been mentored. In terms of external influences, your role as a mentor will be defined by the overarching standards for children's learning, development and care contained within the EYFS (DCSF, 2008a), together with the associated shift towards multidisciplinary provision of integrated services (Savage and Leeson, 2007). Other significant national policies influencing your role include the reform of the levels of training and professional development within the Early Years workforce (CWDC: 2007a) and initiatives regarding the quality of services provided for children and their families (Mitchell, 2007). It is important to recognise the political, social and economic climate in which Early Years practice is situated: this moulds our culture and impacts highly on the manner in which children realise their early experiences (Dana and Yendol-Hoppey, 2005).

At a local level, your understanding of supporting and mentoring others should encompass a wide-ranging conception of this role. We have already identified [in Chapter 4] that the way your role as an EYP develops will be substantially dependent on contextual factors relating to the individual circumstances in which you operate as a leader of practice. For example, you may have responsibility to mentor a practitioner undertaking professional training, which requires specific tasks to be accomplished. Therefore, your mentoring practice should be constructed and interpreted flexibly, though in broad terms there are clearly facets of the role which are generic and requisite.

> *Mentoring in the early years is a dynamic system of advice and support in the context of ongoing professional training and development which makes sense of reflective practice.*

(Callan, 2006: 10)

This definition helps us to conceptualise the EYP's responsive and evolving provision of support for an individual within an environment which is rooted in professional learning and reflection. Further perspective of the role is provided by Rodd (2006: 172), who proposes that mentoring of others by early childhood leaders should be viewed not as 'a supervisory relationship' but as a 'special ongoing personal relationship with that person which is based on the development of rapport, mutual trust, respect and openness to learning'. This suggests the need for the mentor to determine a sensitive, respectful and flexible connection with the individual. What emerges from this understanding of the role is the potential for you, as a mentor, to mutually benefit from the mentoring relationship.

In constructing a perception of the role, you should also consider some specific skills and behaviours that are demonstrated in the process of supporting and mentoring others. These include the ability to:

- demonstrate professional expertise and model effective practice;

- listen actively and provide open, constructive feedback;

- prioritise opportunities for professional dialogue and organise your time for managing mentoring conversations;

- communicate clearly and ensure there is mutual understanding;

- include open questions and clarify any misconceptions;

- acknowledge the significance of non-verbal communication within the mentoring process. Ensure your own non-verbal communication supports mentoring conversations;

- appreciate different learning styles and consider various approaches;

- promote reflection, positive thinking, enquiry and investigation;

- encourage practitioners to be innovative when seeking to find realistic solutions;

- identify opportunities for practitioners to gain experience and deepen their understanding of effective practice;

- suggest additional support that is available and accessible for the practitioner;

- promote the practitioners' confidence and self-esteem;

- offer practitioners encouragement to take on more responsibility and initiative for their own development.

(Adapted from CUREE, 2005)

Within your responsibility for supporting and mentoring others, it is also useful to examine the role of coaching, which focuses on developing specific aspects of practice. According to Callan (2006: 14), coaching is an aspect of Early Years mentoring activity; a coach 'responds to short-term skill-based needs' and will 'encourage, equip and enable others to increase their skills'. A coach working with practitioners in an Early Years setting will assist them with developing their professional competencies within a specified timescale (Rodd, 2006). A mentoring relationship, therefore, differs from coaching in that it is developed over a longer term and mentors are usually more experienced than the mentee. Mentoring is generally centred on the professional development of the mentee, whereas coaching is focused on enabling the mentee to achieve specified areas or issues of development (Connor and Pokora, 2007).

As you reflect on the mentoring role, examine the following case studies and carry out the associated activities below.

CASE STUDY

Ros, an EYP in a children's centre

Ros is mentoring Ellie, a practitioner running a weekly support group for parents and carers. Ellie had recognised that members of the group were interested in using some story boxes at home. While on a local authority course on 'Using Stories', Ellie had developed the boxes, which contained interactive, multi-sensory props to use alongside story sessions and she had demonstrated their use with the group. She thought that if the parents and carers made some story boxes in the group sessions for children to take home, this would help to develop closer links with the group and be beneficial for the children; however, she was unsure how to proceed. Ros encouraged Ellie to examine some options for developing a group project on producing story box resources and summarised the key points at the end of the discussion. Ros arranged to meet with Ellie in the following week to review these points, consider any further concerns and develop an action plan.

These were some of the questions Ros explored with Ellie during their discussion.

- *Do you plan to involve the children in the project and would their interests be taken into account when selecting stories?*

- *How might other practitioners be engaged in this work and how do you think this project could be related to the wider practice of the setting?*

- *Do we need to ensure that resources are safely returned and have you considered who might have responsibility for maintaining the resources?*

- *Have you thought about obtaining feedback on the project and, if so, how do you anticipate that feedback can be collected and used to inform future development?*

Using these questions in the conversation helped to acknowledge and tackle initial concerns about the project. Different options were then openly explored to locate strategies to facilitate its implementation. Future meetings and review of progress would involve practitioner reflection and stakeholder feedback to aid review of the project and highlight possible modifications that may be required.

REFLECTIVE TASK

Consider how Ros supported Ellie and facilitated the development of an action plan for the project. Refer to the groups of Standards for EYPS and note any particular Standards which you think are pertinent to this case study. Look out for links between Standards, 'as, for example, the knowledge and understanding outlined in the first six Standards will inform all aspects of effective practice' (CWDC, 2007a: 4).

Now consider how, as his mentor, you might respond to Amerjit, the practitioner in the next scenario.

Amerjit, a practitioner in a children's centre

Amerjit, your mentee, runs a weekly support session for local childminders in a children's centre. As a key worker for a group of children under two years, he has been developing the use of heuristic play materials and now wishes to extend this work with the group of childminders. Amerjit arranges to meet with you; he has a few queries and would like to talk through his ideas.

Note any key points that are relevant to a discussion on developing Amerjit's initiative, including any particular challenges or responsibilities that will need to be tackled. Then write down some strategies that you might explore with Amerjit and separate these under the headings 'organisational' and 'personal' (Callan, 2006: 10). An example of each type of strategy is given in Table 7.2.

Table 7.2 Examples of organisational and personal strategies

Strategic category	Example of strategy
Organisational	Plan a meeting with the childminders to introduce the heuristic play materials
Personal	Reflect on the children's learning when using the heuristic play materials

---

The strategies that you have explored in the earlier reflective task will help you to develop solutions to a range of issues; however, their real effectiveness will depend upon the contextual factors of the mentoring relationship between mentor and mentee. These factors include communication, emotions and ethics, which will now be considered in the following section.

Factors which can impact on the mentoring process

The mentoring process is dynamic and complex and your role will be contextual; therefore it is important to consider some influential factors in relation to practice within your setting.

Communication

Successful leadership in the early childhood field is a matter of communication more than anything else.

(Rodd, 2006: 65).

The significance of effective communication for the role of EYP has already been identified; it cannot be overstated and indeed is crucial for the mentoring process. It is, therefore, necessary for you to examine aspects of communication that apply specifically to your role as a mentor.

One of the skills which is generic to your work and fundamental to meeting the Standards for EYPs is 'the ability to relate to, and communicate with, others' (CWDC, 2007b: 9). In demonstrating this skill, you are expected to:

- communicate clearly, both in oral and written forms;
- listen to the concerns of others and respond in an appropriate manner;
- display respect and sensitivity towards others;
- manage your personal feelings and needs. (Adapted from CWDC, 2007b: 9)

These skills are further explored in the following task.

REFLECTIVE TASK

From their study of leadership practice within Early Years settings, Siraj-Blatchford and Manni (2007: 15) propose that effective communication is 'Multi-functional and multi-directional; it involves speaking, encouraging, listening, reflecting, translating, interpreting, consulting, debating, summarising, understanding, acknowledging and verifying'.

Reflect on the above definition and highlight any actions contained within the above description that you think are more important for you to use in your practice. Can you add to this description? Note any aspects of communication you would like to develop and any potential barriers to effective communication with practitioners within your own setting.

When communication skills are effectively enacted and applied, clear channels of communication can be created which provide '*transparency* with regard to expectations, practices and processes' (Siraj-Blatchford and Manni, 2007: 15). This clarity enables practitioners to deepen their relationships, which in turn enhances the mentoring process. The result is reflective conversations that can promote feelings of real achievement and empowerment (Rodd, 2006). Reflective conversations are an essential aspect of the mentoring process; professional dialogue promotes a sharing of interpretations of practice, which then provokes further learning and the development of professional knowledge (Ghaye and Ghaye, 1998). By developing more effective communication within your mentoring practice, you can promote an open, reflective approach to Early Years practice. This is particularly significant when we recall, for example, the findings of the studies of *Effective Provision of Pre-School Education (EPPE)* (Sylva et al., 2004) and *Researching Effective Pedagogy in the Early Years (REPEY)* (Siraj-Blatchford et al., 2002), which have demonstrated that 'a more thoughtful, structured approach to everyday activities (derived from sound pedagogical principles) in pre-schools leads to better cognitive and linguistic outcomes for children' (Sylva et al., 2007: 63).

Social/cultural factors

> *It will be a strength in any Early Years mentoring system if it allows appreciation of the learner's unique context and makes use of situational factors to further the most immediate and relevant areas for development and change.*
>
> (Murray, 2006: 64).

Social and cultural factors can influence and may even constrain the EYP in the leadership role; this is particularly true of mentoring relationships. As a mentor, you should be mindful of 'cultural capital' (Edwards, 2000), which denotes the expertise and existing principles applied by practitioners when making professional decisions. Therefore, advice provided by mentors will be inherently influenced by their views and beliefs and you should aim to support practitioners in making informed choices by being 'contextually literate' (Southworth, 2004; see also Siraj-Blatchford and Manni, 2007). As you consider the above points, complete the following reflective activity.

REFLECTIVE TASK

Reflect on the cultural values and beliefs in your early childhood setting which could influence your mentoring practice. Could these values and beliefs support or hinder your work as a mentor? As an EYP, what steps could you take to accommodate the viewpoints of mentees, which may challenge your existing principles?

It is important for you not only to reflect on issues regarding your position within mentoring practice at an individual level but also to consider how mentoring can transform the social and cultural context of your workplace. Developing genuine and open relationships through your mentoring role will support your ability to lead practice by not only promoting individual practitioners' learning but also developing the capacity for this learning to be applied to the wider sphere of the setting and beyond (Murray, 2006). Learning is then located within a social context and therefore, as a mentor, you can promote the development of a 'community of practice' (Lave and Wenger, 1991) whereby 'the culture will become one where learning, self-development and the development of others through reflective conversations is the norm' (Aubrey, 2007: 80). The notion of a 'community of practice' is useful for you to explore because it implies a more holistic approach to your mentoring role, involving collaborative enquiry and a dynamic provision of complementary professional support and advice.

Emotional factors

There is currently an upsurge in interest in all matters emotional and affective in education.

(Hawkey, 2006: 137)

In the last chapter we noted the current focus on emotional issues, such as the interest in the concept of emotional intelligence (Goleman, 1996) and the importance of recognising this dimension of teamwork. You should be aware of how you manage emotional issues that can impact on your mentoring practice – see the reflective task below. Such 'emotional literacy' is identified as 'the practice of recognising, understanding, appropriately expressing and managing emotions in oneself and other people' (Bubb, 2005: 29) and is a key aspect of the mentoring role.

REFLECTIVE TASK

Reflect on emotional factors within your practice and consider the emotional pressures that practitioners may face in the Early Years workplace. What impact could emotional factors have on your mentoring practice? Consider how they might be tackled and resolved.

Understanding and managing your own emotions will enable you to gain more control of these emotions and recognise emotions in others. Mentoring activity, with its capacity for nurturing individuals, can be viewed as an 'intensely human activity with learning at its heart' (Garvey, 1999: 42). As you recognise the impact and implications of emotional factors for your mentoring role, you should also explore the need proposed by Megginson et al. (2006: 253) for mentors to exhibit 'empathetic curiosity', which is the 'ability to demonstrate interest in the other as a person, while being sensitive to his or her concerns and emotions'.

Figure 7.1 illustrates the 'emotional climate' in the workplace that can influence practitioners' feelings and affect their performance.

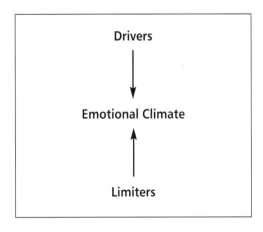

Figure 7.1 Emotional climate and performance (adapted from Rhodes et al., 2004: 102)

This diagram demonstrates how emotions, such as optimism, can 'drive' performance, whereas feelings of anxiety can 'limit' performance (Rhodes et al., 2004: 102). By influencing the 'emotional climate' in the workplace, you can motivate practitioners and develop their performance.

REFLECTIVE TASK

Consider emotional 'drivers' and 'limiters' within your setting. How could you could increase 'drivers' and decrease 'limiters' through your mentoring practice?

Trust

Individual mentoring requires the establishment of appropriate and agreed ground-rules in the context of a trusting relationship.

(Aubrey, 2007: 82)

The importance of the trustworthiness of the EYP was explored earlier and has already been identified as a key dimension to effective teamwork. Within the mentoring relationship, too, the way trust is built and maintained is critical. This will encourage practitioners to share and discuss their ideas, including any concerns they may have relating to their practice. Therefore, it is important to demonstrate that you value practitioners' efforts and demonstrate traits of honesty and sincerity which will promote confidence in the mentoring relationship and process.

We have already considered briefly the potentially damaging influence of hierarchical structures within teams and the possible negative effect on practitioners' self-esteem. Rodd (2006: 173) warns that mentees may become compliant through the 'perceived powers of mentors' and suggests that mentors should create a 'supportive framework' and clarify 'goals and obligations' with their mentees. Therefore, in order to promote effective relationships, you should consider developing a mentoring practice that is based on collaboration. Such a model of 'collaborative mentoring' (Callan and Copp, 2006: 18) should be grounded on the fundamental principles of 'confidentiality, credibility and clarity, all of which engender trust between those involved'. The issue of trust is explored further in the case study below.

CASE STUDY

Marsha, an EYP in a private nursery

Marsha, whose setting has limited outdoor access, was discussing plans for a visit to a local park with Eva, a practitioner who had recently joined the setting. Marsha, referring to the EYFS guidance on play (DCSF, 2008b), explained how these outings had proved very beneficial for the children in the past. Despite the enthusiasm Eva normally displayed when working with the children, she seemed very reticent about this visit. In the course of the conversation Eva then explained that she had felt quite scared of dogs since she was a child and was therefore worried in case she encountered any dogs during the outing to the park. If this happened, Eva was concerned that the children might sense her anxiety.

As well as empathising with Eva's concerns and reassuring her about health and safety procedures for the impending setting visit, Marsha then suggested some strategies which could help Eva to feel more secure about accompanying children on outings. Though Eva was keen to overcome her apprehension about outings, Marsha recognised that other staff would need to be involved in tackling the issue, so she then sought and gained Eva's consent to discuss this matter with them.

REFLECTIVE TASK

- *What are the important considerations relating to Marsha and Eva in this mentoring conversation?*

- *Are there any specific skills and behaviours that you think Marsha applied in this scenario?*

- *Consider how you can build mutual respect and trust to promote greater feelings of security and confidence within a mentoring relationship. What barriers might you encounter?*

One of Marsha's key considerations was confidentiality. In managing this issue as a mentor, you will need to consider the same principles as those applying to effective teamwork. If confidential issues are to be discussed, then access to an appropriate place for mentoring conversations, where both the mentor and practitioner feel secure and relaxed, is helpful. However, where space in the setting is limited, finding a suitable location may prove to be more challenging. It is beneficial to consider the use of appropriate spaces for mentoring conversations, which do not have a negative impact for others in the setting.

Ethical conduct

Having a clear understanding of the ethics of mentoring – both in general and in how they apply to the specific mentoring relationship – is important.

(Megginson et al., 2006: 33)

As you reflect on your role as a mentor, it is also pertinent to consider ethical conduct. This involves adhering to agreed moral values and principles, which are designed to support safe and effective mentoring practice (Connor and Pokora, 2007).

Both mentor and mentee should share a common understanding of their approach to the mentoring relationship, display positive attitudes towards the mentoring process and have mutual respect for each other. You should refer to ethical codes provided by professional associations, which offer guidance to underpin practice; these can be helpful in developing internal frameworks that will be recognised by all participants and situated within the overarching policies and procedures that apply to the setting as a whole.

Although not specifically aimed at mentoring within Early Years settings, the following checklist provides some useful points for reflection in respect of ethical conduct:

- responsibilities to others;

- conflicts in priorities, especially regarding confidentiality;

- boundaries to remain within;

- appropriate levels of personal intimacy;

- view on withdrawal from a relationship;

- position on allowing a mentee to fail;

- approach to pushing mentees towards what you know they require instead of what they state they need ;

- attitude to withholding information from the mentee. (Adapted from Megginson et al., 2006: 34)

REFLECTIVE TASK

Consider your attitude towards establishing boundaries within a mentoring relationship. Reflect on any possible concerns for either the mentor or mentee about the following:

- *physical contact;*

- *self-disclosure;*

- *receipt of gifts;*

- *personal space.*

(Adapted from Barnett, 2008)

Time

> *Demands on the time of the mentor affect effectiveness.*
> (Stephenson and Sampson, 1994: 186)

As mentoring can be a time-consuming activity, a key consideration for developing effective mentoring experiences will be efficient time management. You should consider your availability when agreeing to mentor a colleague and ensure that you both concur with mentoring arrangements so that there is clarity about shared commitment to the process (Aubrey, 2007). Though you will need to demonstrate your genuine readiness to offer your time, mentoring should not impact on personal time for you or the practitioner.

You should aim to develop reasonable timescales regarding arrangements within your mentoring practice which enable practitioners to have secure and realistic expectations about the process. For example, the nature of work in Early Years settings involves a 'duty of care' and mentoring arrangements may need to be modified in order primarily to manage the needs of the children (Rodd, 2006: 91). Finding common time in a demanding schedule can be challenging but you could, for example, use existing opportunities for mentoring conversations, such as shared planning time.

Though circumstances affecting time for mentoring will sometimes be outside your control, it is nevertheless useful to identify some strategies for effective time management to assist you with your mentoring role. One such activity, suggested by Rodd (2006: 93), is included in the following task.

REFLECTIVE TASK

Consider how you manage your time; then complete your typical daily schedule using the following list of general headings. Add any further headings that you think you should include – this list should be relevant to your own practice and schedules:

- *things to do;*
- *people to see;*
- *phone calls to make;*
- *meetings to attend;*
- *deadlines to meet.*

This task will help you to establish effective time management and focus your awareness on the pressures on your time.

Figure 7.2 summarises the key factors covered in this section.

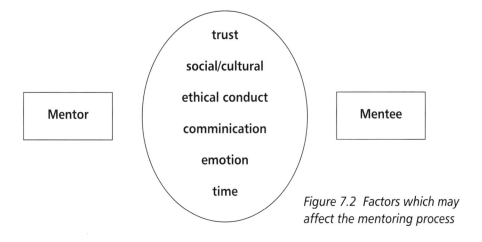

Figure 7.2 Factors which may affect the mentoring process

Effectiveness as a mentor

Because early years work relies on the development of strong and successful relationships, this is a profession in which the quality of the outcomes can be directly tied to the quality of the people working with them.

(Owen, 2006: 194)

As you develop your role as a mentor, you will need to consider how you can evaluate your practice. Mentees themselves will provide useful indicators of your effectiveness so you should think about how their feedback could be obtained and analysed to facilitate evaluation of your mentoring. Other colleagues who are familiar with your mentoring practice may act in the role of the critical friend (Bush and Middlewood, 2005) and provide useful feedback, as well as sharing reflections and exploring mentoring issues.

Your ability to reflect on your mentoring role is a powerful tool and will help you to identify areas of practice that you feel are more successful and those that may require greater focus. Indicators of successful mentoring include:

- changes in behaviour and improvements to practice;

- increased satisfaction and motivation;

- decreased stress;

- changes in attitudes, empowerment to act and longer-term impact;

- impact or influence on others, in the setting and beyond;

- sustained quality improvement. (Adapted from Murray, 2006: 73)

It is also useful to consider some limitations of mentoring, such as when mentors:

- have their own agendas;

- encourage practitioners to replicate themselves;

- promote dependency;

- maintain the status quo;

- lack time for effectively managing their role;

- ignore the challenge of an unsuitable 'match' with their mentee.

(Adapted from Bush and Middlewood, 2005: 167–8)

REFLECTIVE TASK

Consider how you evaluate your effectiveness as a mentor.

- *Are any of the above limitations of mentoring practice applicable to you?*

- *What could you do to enhance your role as a mentor?*

Mentoring can be a mutually supportive process leading to improved relationships and new understandings (Rodd, 2006); you should therefore also assess the experiential impact on the development and application of your own knowledge as a result of your mentoring role (S38, S39). Even if you feel that your mentoring experience has been valuable and effective, it is important that you are nurtured and provided with ongoing support and opportunities for professional development (Garvey and Alred, 2000).

Personal and shared reflection on mentoring experiences and feedback from others will help you to consider how any tensions within practice could be resolved and to develop a dynamic combination of skills to promote effective approaches to your mentoring practice. This will enable you to extend the capacity to undertake your mentoring role within a range of Early Years settings and adapt to future developments in policy and practice.

REFLECTIVE TASK

Now reflect on the skills that you could utilise to support the development of a practitioner in your setting. Note any resources that could be required, including support from other practitioners who may be involved. Consider any skills you may need to develop so that you can provide effective mentoring.

C H A P T E R S U M M A R Y

In this chapter we have considered the knowledge, skills, behaviours and attitudes required by an EYP in the role of mentor and drawn on a number of theoretical sources to illustrate these, particularly the work of Callan (2006). You have considered the concept of mentoring as a significant example of leading practice and have reflected on how to develop effective mentor/mentee relationships in your own setting and the impact these can have on the quality of provision and practice.

Moving on

In the next chapter, we turn our attention to what makes for effective and successful partnership working. We will reflect on how the EYP works in partnership with families, within multi-professional teams within the setting and with agencies/other professionals external to the setting. The notion of the EYP as a collaborative leader is explored further as this is identified as best fitting the way you should lead partnership practice.

Self-assessment task

In this chapter you have had the opportunity to reflect on the attitudes, knowledge and skills that are required within the mentoring process. Use the following activity to apply your learning to help inform your understanding of areas of strengths as well as development in the mentoring role. It would be particularly useful to carry out this exercise in collaboration with a colleague (see Chapter 5) or even with a mentee.

Table 7.3 Strengths and areas for development in the mentoring role

	Strengths	Areas for development
Knowledge: • of the nature of the mentor/mentee relationship (pages 109–110) • of contextual factors (social and cultural) affecting the role (pages 112–116) • of the mentor as 'coach' (page 110) Skills: • active listening • effective oral communication • understanding of non-verbal cues • promotion of reflection and enquiry • model effective practice • nurture mentor's confidence and self-esteem (see CUREE, 2005 on page 110) Attitudes: • trust in the mentor/mentee relationship • the importance of confidentiality • the ethical dimensions of the role of mentor • to time management (pages 116–119)		

FURTHER READING

Robbins, A. (ed.) (2006) *Mentoring in the Early Years.* London: Sage (Chapters 1 and 2).

8 The Early Years Professional working in partnership

CHAPTER OBJECTIVES

In this chapter we identify key factors in effective and successful partnership working: with families; within different professionals within a setting; and with external agencies. There is discussion around engagement and involvement with these partners in Early Years practice. In focusing on the role of the leader of practice, we consider ways of helping colleagues to work more effectively with parents/families and with other agencies. The reflective tasks and self-assessment exercises aim to support you in leading and enabling a collaborative approach to improving practice and developing collective accountability.

After reading this chapter you should be able to:
- identify key factors that contribute to effective team engagement with families;
- reflect on the importance of professional collaboration with other professionals both within and external to the setting;
- appraise critically your own strengths and areas for development in leading partnership practice;
- apply your understanding to the preparation of your evidence for EYP validation.

This chapter focuses specifically on EYP Standards 3, 6, 29, 30, 31, 32 and 36 but you are encouraged to reflect broadly across the other Standards as you seek to apply your knowledge, understanding and skills in partnership work to all aspects of your practice.

Introduction

In their 2007 study, *Effective Leadership in the Early Years (ELEYS)*, Siraj-Blatchford and Manni identify one of the fundamental requirements for the leadership role in early childhood as a commitment to collaboration. This is where 'effective pedagogic and parental support are complementary and where there are strong inter-agency partnerships' (Siraj-Blatchford and Manni, 2007: 12).

Over the past decade or so, we have seen an increasing movement towards integrated working with children and young people: a multi-professional, collaborative approach. The rationale for this is soundly based on a belief that, where everyone works together effectively to put the child at the centre, then the child's needs will be met and her life improved (CWDC, 2007d). The EYP Standards reflect strongly this emphasis on integrated delivery, with a whole section devoted to collaboration with families (S29–32), and some explicitly relating to effective working with other professionals (particularly S6, S36).

In this chapter, we focus firstly on the role of the EYP in developing and leading strong partnerships with families and carers and then move to consider the role within a multi-agency context. Bronfenbrenner's (1979) seminal ecological model of human development offers a clear theoretical framework for our discussion (see Figure 8.1). This model, with the child at the centre, considers the different 'systems' to which the child is connected, each system influencing the other in a two-way state of reciprocal change (Garbarino, 1992). The child is both influenced by and directly influences her/his environment. For instance, although a particular child is unlikely to meet Government policy makers, it can be argued that social policy is driven largely by the needs of families, which in turn reflect the needs of individual children. The thrust of Bronfenbrenner's argument is that societies should place a high value on responding to the needs of young children but that this can only be achieved when 'members of that society acknowledge the complex inter-relationship between children, parents, educators, carers, community groups and those responsible for key services' (Anning and Edwards, 2006: 3) It is the EYP's role to recognise and acknowledge these complex inter-relationships and lead others to develop effective partnerships.

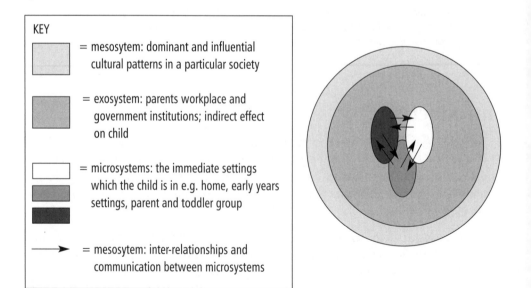

KEY

= mesosytem: dominant and influential cultural patterns in a particular society

= exosystem: parents workplace and government institutions; indirect effect on child

= microsystems: the immediate settings which the child is in e.g. home, early years settings, parent and toddler group

⟶ = mesosytem: inter-relationships and communication between microsystems

Figure 8.1 Bronfenbrenner's ecological model of human development

The child in the family context

We all have associated images when we think of a 'family unit' but contemporary society is hugely diverse and families now take a very wide range of forms. The principles of equality practice considered earlier apply here, too, and as an EYP you will have significant responsibility in seeking to understand the needs of different families in your setting. These will include mothers, fathers, step-parents, other carers, grandparents, siblings, other members of the wider family and so on. The approach to all families should be one of empathy, care and professionalism. Dwiveldi (1996) suggests that is virtually impossible for any professional to be fully knowledgeable about the different contexts of all children but that it should be possible to be open to learning from children and their families about those differences. This makes an important point above about both the limitations and the possibilities for the EYP in learning from and supporting families. This is indeed a two-way reciprocal process (Bronfenbrenner, 1979).

In 2007 the Government department responsible for education was reformed into two distinct, new departments. The establishment of the Department for Children, Schools and Families (DCSF) symbolised a more holistic stance on and understanding of children's lives. The production of the Children's Plan (DCSF, 2007b: 5), building on a decade of earlier reform and setting out further strategic targets to improve outcomes for children by 2020, is added evidence that the state believes 'families are the bedrock of society and the place for nurturing happy, capable and resilient children'. In preparing the Children's Plan the Government had consulted widely with families and noted that they would like 'better and more flexible information from all service providers and support that better reflects the lives we lead'. The consultation further emphasised how important it is that parents are involved with policy affecting children and that 'we need particularly to improve how government and services involve fathers more effectively' (DCSF, 2007b: 5).

History will judge if this lofty rhetoric becomes reality, especially given the increasingly ill-defined boundary between state and family responsibility (Millar, 2008) but for the EYP, the new emphasis on effective pedagogy and professionalism within Early Years provision and practice are important steps. As an EYP you will need to be aware of the complexities of family partnership and yet remain positive about the possibilities offered by them and seek to support and lead colleagues in this aspect of equality practice.

REFLECTIVE TASK

Establishing an active and equal and relationship with parents depends on a setting having clear values.

(Pen Green Team, 2007)

- *How do you view your role as EYP in contributing to your setting's values on family partnerships and the ethos that is created?*

- *In your reflections, are you aware of any personal experiences and views of 'family' that might weaken your equality practice in this area? What might you do about this?*

REFLECTIVE TASK CONTINUED

- *What responsibility do you have of leading practice in establishing reciprocal relationships with different types of families in your setting?*

- *How might you strengthen partnership with fathers in your setting?*

As we have discussed, one of the four themes of the EYFS is that of 'positive relationships' and this includes positive relationships with families. There are excellent resources on the EYFS CD-ROM to support your reflections on your own practice here; one is highlighted towards the end of this chapter. Rodd (2006) suggests that there are three strands to parental involvement in Early Years provision and practice: partnership, continuity and education. We consider each of these in turn and you should use the opportunity to reflect on the range of EYP Standards which can be applied to successful collaboration with families and carers, including those that focus on effective practices (S7–24). Specifically, though, it is S3, 29, 30, 31 and 32 which directly embrace the multi-faceted nature of this aspect of the EYP role. In particular:

- the significance of transitions from home to setting (S3);

- the role of families in children's learning, development and well-being (S29);

- the importance of constructive relationships and effective communication (S30);

- the need for collaboration to improve outcomes for children (S31);

- two-way sharing of information about children's achievements and progress (S32).

(Based on CWDC, 2007a)

Consider the following accounts from three different EYPs of how they work with parents.

Example 1 – Georgia, manager of a private day nursery:

'I try to reflect continuously on everything I do from the day-to-day detail to contributing to the overall ethos of the setting. In consultation with the families and staff, we decided that the best time for open days would be weekend afternoons and these worked really well. We often take a specific aspect of learning as our theme – such as support for communication, language and literacy or problem solving, reasoning and numeracy – and our parents have found this really helpful. Of course, this is all underpinned by effective daily two-way communication between families and the key persons.'

Example 2 – Pamela, a registered childminder:

'I believe my role as EYP is to lead by providing examples of good practice, engaging in professional development to improve and update my own understanding of practice. It is fundamental to my role that I engage effectively with the families of the children in my charge. I meet with all parents before their child starts with me and ask them to complete an "All About Me" form which provides me with as much essential information about the children as possible. This enables me to provide a familiar, comfortable setting when they start. I listen carefully to parents' comments and use these in the children's profiles where appropriate.'

Example 3 – Sharon, Early Years teacher attached to a private nursery setting:

'I believe my role is to develop the practice of myself and others in implementing new initiatives and ideas that improve outcomes for the children in my setting. Legislation offering longer periods of parental leave resulted in fewer very young babies starting at the nursery; so we discussed with parents the possibility of starting Parent and Baby sessions in the nursery prior to parents returning to work and babies starting in the nursery. These groups included opportunity for support and professional advice to parents who requested it and the sessions were very well received, especially as they made for very smooth transitions between home and nursery.'

REFLECTIVE TASK

Look in the Guidance to the Standards for the Award of EYPS (CWDC, 2007a) at EYP Standards 3, 29, 30, 31 and 32. Then reflect on these three accounts from practitioners.

- *How might Georgia, Pamela and Sharon map their accounts here to the different Standards?*

- *Continue to reflect on the possibilities you have for effective two-way collaboration with families and the evidence you might use.*

- *What are the specific challenges for you as leader of practice here?*

Partnership

The concept of a 'triangle of care', a partnership between parents and professional, has been around since the 1994 Start Right Report (Ball, 1994). This recognised that one of the key tasks of Early Years practitioners was to establish strong partnerships with parents as the child's 'first and most enduring educators' (DFEE, 2000). Since then, this has been identified as a principal practice issue in a number of research reports (Bertram and Pascal, 2002; Siraj-Blatchford et al., 2002; Sylva et al., 2004).

The pioneering work of the Reggio Emilia pre-schools in Italy was discussed in Chapter 5. Their view of pedagogy, which places families at the heart of an alliance of practitioners, the community – including local artists – and policy makers (Abbott and Nutbrown, 2001) has been highly influential in our understanding of contemporary practice and there have been many flagship settings exemplifying effective partnership working, such as the Thomas Coram Centre in London. The practice of and research into the involvement of parents in their children's learning at the Pen Green Centre, Northampton (Whalley et al., 2007) has proved particularly inspiring to many Early Years practitioners in identifying innovative partnership working in their own settings. Pen Green is set in a socially challenging area but since the 1980s, staff have been committed to 'engaging parents as decision-makers in the planning and implementation of work at the centre' and by the late 1990s a culture was in place in which 'children, parents and staff were encouraged to share decision-making, able to question, challenge and make choices' (Whalley et al., 2007: 7). The outcomes for children and families at Pen Green have been remarkable and embrace all three of Rodd's (2006) themes: partnership, continuity and education. Conclusions drawn from the action research into partnerships with parents at Pen Green include the recognition of:

1. the great untapped energy and ability of parents and their deep commitment to supporting their children's development;

2. the importance of developing a mutual understanding based on shared experiences;

3. the need to have a clearly articulated pedagogical approach – where professional are clear about their own beliefs and can then share these with parents;

4. the need for staff to be as enthusiastic about working with adults, including parents, as with children;

5. the time needed to establish equal, active and responsible partnerships with parents;

6. parents getting involved in their own time, at their own pace and in their own way;

7. the political dimension of working with families where parents 'stop accepting their lot and start creating the world they'd like to be part of' (Pascal, 1996: 2, cited in Whalley et al., 2007: 32).

REFLECTIVE TASK

Look again at the conclusions drawn from the findings of the Pen Green staff above.

- *Do any of these surprise you?*

- *Focus particularly on points 4, 5, 6 and 7. How do you see these connecting to the EYP Standards – especially S3, 29, 30, 31 and 32?*

- *Are you able to identify particular strengths in this area of your own practice?*

- *What particular opportunities and challenges do you face in leading others in understanding the importance of partnership with families?*

Whilst the idea that parents should play a major role in their children's learning now passes virtually uncontested, any family involvement must be at the family's own pace and way. EYPs should be alert to this and aware of both the potential and the real pressures on families. Many succumb to the seductive pressure of the market in purchasing expensive (and arguably unnecessary) pre-school 'learning' resources. Such parents may question the approach to EYFS provision which does not use such materials. Others, facing huge domestic, financial or work-related difficulties, may feel they have limited energy to give to 'supporting' their child's learning in the way that many of our Early Years settings now expect. This is a complex issue and time and space prevent further discussion but, conceivably, demanding that parents turn themselves into 'teachers' might actually widen rather than narrow the gap between families (Karpf, 2007). Consider the following conversation between two parents: Dilip, a pharmacist and father of three-year-old Rajata, and Hyacinth, a part-time librarian and mother of three-year-old Lloyd. Rajata and Lloyd both go to the same nursery and are friends.

Hyacinth to Dilip: 'Have you read this month's (nursery) newsletter yet?'

Dilip: 'No, I haven't had time yet.'

Hyacinth: 'The nursery's going to introduce a new reading programme called "Fantastic Phonemes". It looks really exciting and they're going to organise a parents' session, probably on a Saturday morning so we can take the children, too.'

Dilip: 'I work on Saturday mornings so I don't think I'll be able to go.'

Hyacinth: 'I really think it's brilliant that they're going for this. I'm getting Lloyd a computer program for Christmas that will encourage him to learn the alphabet.'

Dilip: 'Rajata loves stories and I wish I had more time to read to her but I think she's a bit young to be learning the alphabet.'

Hyacinth: 'I don't think they're ever too young. My sister's little girl is in Year 2 now and is struggling a bit to keep up. I don't want that to happen to Lloyd.'

Dilip: 'I don't want to think too much about school. Rajata has only just stopped being a baby and is enjoying her days at nursery so much. She talks about Mandy [key person] all the time at home.'

Hyacinth: 'Well, I hope you've got her name down for the Big'Un Primary School because it's ever so popular and they'll be five in no time.'

REFLECTIVE TASK

Although this is an imaginary conversation, these two parents do represent sincerely held parental views of a child's Early Years. Think about the following.

- *the ethos promoted in your setting and how this might be interpreted by both the 'Hyacinths' and the 'Dilips';*

- *how your setting conveys the notion of 'involvement in learning' to parents;*

- *your role in leading others in this aspect of practice.*

Continuity

Beyond dispute, one area of crucial importance in the home/setting partnership is that of managing children's transitions. EYP S3 recognises the significance of transitions for young children:

- as children enter into an Early Years setting for the first time;

- within settings from one base area to another;

- across settings, where geographical mobility and flexible working patterns often result in children moving from one area to another or where childcare is simultaneously shared by two or more providers;

- from an Early Years setting to a school setting.

Here effective collaboration, especially between families and key persons (see Chapter 5), is crucial if we are to achieve smooth continuity and progression for each child. It is an accepted truth within our understanding of children's development that the younger the child the more important this is, but this is not to underestimate the significance of transitions for older children, too; and as noted, this is now reflected in the statutory requirement (DfES, 2007a) for all children within the EYFS to have a designated key person who is the first point of contact between family and setting.

Drawing on key research by David et al. (2003) and Trevarthen (2001) related to children under three, Langston (2006) describes how, in optimum circumstances, parents provide for their young: 'emotional nurture; social companionship; cognitive and language stimulation; and appropriate care to promote their physical and mental health and well being' (Langston, 2006: 9). These are all fundamental to healthy human development; the importance of the key person/child/family triangular relationship in constructing these for the child cannot be overemphasised. Two EYPs share their experience here.

CASE STUDY

Carrolle (a registered childminder who currently has two siblings in her charge, Martha, aged four, and Daniel aged two)

'Martha and Daniel are very settled with me but next week, James, aged 10 months, is joining us on three days. James is the younger of two but his older sister is now at school. I minded his sister, Nia, too and she always settled well. James is strongly attached to his mum, Sara, who is only reluctantly returning to work following maternity leave. Sara and James have called in weekly for the last few weeks and last week, James stayed on his own for two hours. He was very distressed when Sara left and I could see that she was tearful too! However, he did settle while she was away and enjoyed spectating Daniel's play with the Duplo. Sara was very anxious when she returned and James immediately wanted to go to her but I told her he had settled and been interested in Daniel's play. This week we repeated this, with much the same pattern although he did show interest when we shared a picture book together. I had already spent some time talking to Sara about James' likes, dislikes and routines and also phoned her one evening last week to reassure her that he would soon get into the routine of being dropped off on the days she is working.'

- *In what ways is Carrolle demonstrating the key person relationship here?*

- *Can you identify ways in which Carrolle might strengthen the partnership between herself and Sara?*

Matt is room leader of the 20-place pre-school room (3–4year olds) within a children's centre

'We don't have a fixed point at which children will transfer to our room (upstairs) from the toddlers' (two–three-year-olds) base but, rather, the child's key person will discuss with me and our manager when s/he feels a child is developmentally ready for the move. This usually works very well and we have a system whereby the existing key person will bring the new child up for short sessions over a period of weeks and then come and work with the new key person for a while (according to each child's needs). We believe this creates an important sense of continuity for the child. However, Jemima is now three and a half and although we have tried to include her in the pre-school for short periods of time, she is still very tearful and anxious and her mum, Tara, has asked that she be allowed to stay downstairs for now. We arranged a meeting recently with the manager, Tara, Lenny (Jemima's key person) and myself and all agreed this was in Jemima's best interests at this time. We will review the situation in six weeks.'

- *In what ways is Matt demonstrating skills in leading practice here?*

- *In what ways are staff and parent(s) working collaboratively here in Jemima's best interest?*

- *Can you think of other approaches to leadership in this kind of situation?*

Empowerment and education

Arnold (Whalley et al., 2007: 65) believes that parents are 'experts on the subject of their own children' and can share this expertise with professionals. Equally, she believes it is helpful if professionals 'share specialised language and concepts with parents'.

Much of the 'empowerment' literature relating to parent partnership stems from consideration of the particular needs of families of children with a disability or additional needs (Appleton and Minchom, 1991). In role-modelling an inclusive approach to practice, the EYP will be particularly mindful of the needs of such families. The concept of empowering parents is described by Bax (2001: 291) as a 'move in the right direction' away from former models of understanding the parental/professional partnership, which include:

- the 'expert' model, in which the professional asserts her/his expertise with little awareness of parental 'expertise';

- the 'transplant' model, which rigidly delineates responsibilities at *home* (the parents') and *outside the home* (the professionals');

- the 'consumer rights' model, in which parents are seen as key stakeholders accessing services in a competitive market, and in which the professional needs to 'impress';

- the 'social networks' model, in which parents encouraged to derive strength and support from other parents, especially in similar circumstances.

By contrast, in the 'empowerment' model professionals actively promote parents' sense of control over decisions affecting their child.

Although such models have particular resonance for families where a child has a special educational need, they can be applied equally to engagement with all families. It is the 'empowerment' model to which the EYP aspires, modelling and demonstrating sensitivity to the parents' right to opt into the professional system at any level they choose (Bax, 2001: 291). Indeed, the Sure Start/CWDC children's centre agenda includes this component as part of its core aims/objectives and most children's centres now act as a 'local service hub'/'one stop shop' for families, offering a range of services and provision for parents including family support services, child and family health services and effective links with job centres and local training providers. Early Years settings in the private, voluntary and independent sectors may not be able to offer the same breadth of service but many are finding imaginative ways to 'empower' parents. Look back at Georgia's and Sharon's work in private nurseries (pages 126–127) and how they are working to support parents in specific and manageable ways. Consider now how Emma and Kate are working to empower different parents in their settings:

CASE STUDY

Emma (the owner/leader of a term-time only/school hours private pre-school setting

'Two of the children, Jennie and Luke, in our setting have statements of special educational needs. Jennie's mum, Veronica, has experienced a range of additional challenges, including the break-up of her relationship with Jennie's father, and when Jennie started at the pre-school, Veronica was in a low state of health and very anxious about being

separated from Jennie. I am the pre-school SENCO and Jennie's key person. I worked with Veronica prior to Jennie starting, to build up an initial profile of the child. As we chatted, I learned that Veronica is very interested in pursuing local training opportunities in Early Years practice. With the rest of the staff, I sounded out a suggestion that, subject to CRB enhanced disclosure, Veronica could come in on a voluntary basis one or two sessions a week and be part of our team. Veronica does not have any direct responsibility for her own daughter, Jennie, when she is in but all the staff remark on the positive contribution she is making, especially as we discover she is a confident singer and supports our singing sessions really enthusiastically. She has now enrolled on a course in Early Years practice.'

CASE STUDY

Kate (the proprietor/manager of a private day nursery: although she is super-numerary to staff ratios, Kate has a strong commitment to leading practice and giving a vision to the nursery)

'One of our three-year-old children was really struggling with behaviour issues. It was crucial that I and his key person should meet with the child's parents as soon as possible and the parents were very happy to do so. At this meeting, the parents shared that at home the child is accustomed to telling everyone what to do and having his own way. With the parents, we looked at some key aspects of behaviour management and together we formulated a strategy whereby at both home and nursery, the approach would be for the adult to decide the right response in a given situation and say to the child either "this is your choice" or "this is my choice". This way the child retained many opportunities to make his choice but, on occasions, had to begin to learn that sometimes he could not and to deal with the frustration of this. The parents felt they were recovering some vestige of control in what was increasingly an out-of-control situation.'

REFLECTIVE TASK

These are two different examples of leadership which respond to the specific needs of parents.

- *In what ways did both Emma and Kate demonstrate a collaborative approach to parent partnership here? Was there anything they might have done differently?*

- *How might they use these examples as evidence of their leadership of practice?*

- *Can you identify examples from your own practice of leading practice which empowers parents?*

Multi-agency partnerships

The EYP role also includes leading practice within the context of working with other types of professionals and with agencies external to the setting. Anning and Edwards (2006: 17) describe as an 'imperative' that the approach to meeting the needs of families with young children should be 'joined up' and delivered by professionals working together as part of a multi-agency team. Once more, Bronfenbrenner's (1979) ecological model of child development is relevant here as we reflect on the inter-related nature of family, parent and children's needs in the fields of health, social services, education, law enforcement and housing. Families do not live compartmentalised lives.

The integrated approach to services has also been driven to some extent by the need to make sure children – especially those most in need of it – are accessing the services, care and protection to which they are entitled as part of the 2004 Children Act. The unspeakable tragedy of the Victoria Climbié case and the subsequent inquiry by Lord Laming (Home Office, 2003) has determined a preventative and early intervention agenda in which all professionals working with and for children must work together more collaboratively.

> *All managers in children's services are expected to have and to promote a plan for protecting children from harm and actively promoting their welfare. . . (including the) rights of excluded and under-served groups . . . defining and implementing multi-agency approach to managing risk; and ensuring that the child's voice is not only heard but responded to.*

> (DfES, 2006b: 8)

Overall responsibility for such a task clearly rests with the organisational leader. Indeed the CWDC (2007c) is actively promoting the role of 'lead professional' in integrated service provision and the programme for NPQICL focuses on this dimension of leadership; this is not a new role but includes the coordination of the core functions defined in the delivery of 'a seamless and effective service' (CWDC, 2007e: 1). As EYPs, you should be conversant with the role of 'lead professional' and be ready to make an informed contribution to a multi-agency approach to safeguarding children.

REFLECTIVE TASK

Full integrated service provision is situated within the children's centre and extended schools developments. However, EYP Standards 4 and 5 require you to have a working knowledge of both rationale and procedure relating to national policy within which children's services operate.

- *How do you ensure that you have the most up-to-date information on policy issues relating to multi-agency working?*

- *How do you disseminate this information to colleagues and lead on its impact on practice in your setting?*

- *How does this fit with the requirement on all staff to contribute to the safeguarding of all children?*

- *What particular challenges do you face here and how are you addressing these?*

The Common Assessment Framework (CAF)

This is a key component of the *Every Child Matters: Change for Children* programme (DfES, 2004a) and aims to identify at the earliest possible opportunity any child or young person's additional needs not currently being met. CAF has three distinct elements: a pre-assessment checklist; a process for undertaking common assessment; and a standard proforma to document the assessment.

> *(The CAF) . . . will help embed a shared language; support better understanding amongst practitioners; reduce the number of different assessments; facilitate early interventions; and speed up service delivery.*
>
> (CWDC, 2007f)

The CAF takes a highly holistic approach to assessment but does consider three themes (and, at the time of writing, a national IT system to support it is being developed):

- **the child's development**: health; emotional and social development; behavioural; development; family and social relationships; self-care and independence; and learning;

- **parents and carers**: basic care; emotional stability; and guidance and boundaries;

- **family and environmental**: family history and functioning; wider family; housing and economic factors; and social and community factors.

Anning et al. (2006:127) remind us that what really matters is that the 'delivery of services for children and families is better than it was and results in enhanced outcomes for them'.

REFLECTIVE TASK

Pause for a moment to think about different aspects of your own practice, particularly those which involve working with other professionals. Are you able to trace any 'improvements' in the delivery of services that you support which are resulting in better outcomes for children and families? Make a note of your reflections.

The role of the EYP in inter-professional communication and collaboration

It is in this area that the EYP has a very clear role. Powell (2007: 24) suggests that failure in inter-agency collaboration and communication can occur partly because of a 'lack of desire' to relinquish specific involvement and to accept the need for other professional intervention. Perhaps in the past this has been the case and there remains a residue of such an attitude, but increasingly professionals are recognising that they each have an equal but distinctively different role to play in effective service provision for children and their families. As an EYP you can be confident of the distinctive professional contribution you make through your expertise in specialist knowledge of the principles and content of the EYFS and of child development (Standards 1 and 2). Nonetheless there are challenges here (Anning et al., 2006; Powell, 2007) and potential barriers to effective inter-professional communication and collaboration. These include the following:

- confusion about parameters of roles and responsibilities – especially in working together whilst acknowledging the importance of specialist expertise;

- disappointment and frustration about slowness or lack of change;

- conflicting priorities and work practices;

- little systematic or effective sharing;

- exclusion of others by the use of jargon.

Maryam and Frank share their – very different – experiences below.

CASE STUDY

Maryam, a family support worker in an urban Sure Start local project

'I help run twice weekly parent and children lunchtime groups where a specialist playworker organises a play-based programme for the children, a local catering firm provides a healthy vegetarian snack for all users and one or other of the local team of health visitors tries to pop in. My role is one of outreach into the community to try and encourage those who are otherwise resistant to such groups to make use of the service they offer and then to befriend and "actively listen" to parents while their children play. Often I encourage the parents to play with the children or even to explore the play resources for themselves. Selma, one of the mums, usually loves the playdough but I am concerned about her at the moment as she is increasingly subdued and one of her children, Iqbal, is much more clingy to her and will not go and play independently as he used to. Selma won't talk about anything. I have mentioned it once or twice to the health visitor but got a non-committal response and we don't have the time to get together more formally to share concerns.'

CASE STUDY

Frank, deputy manager of full-day care provision within a children's centre and room leader of two–three-year-olds

'I am three-year-old Lester's key person; he is an only child and lives with dad who is a lone parent. Lester has complex needs, has limited mobility and is not yet using much recognisable language. Since he started at the centre a year ago, I have liaised closely with dad, his (Mencap) family support worker, health visitor and speech and language therapist (SALT). We all meet bi-monthly to review provision for Lester and this has been working well. At the last meeting, the family support worker raised her concerns that dad

is increasingly distracted with work demands and is not spending as much time playing with Lester and nurturing his emotional needs as he used to. Dad felt confident enough to share his own concerns here and the health visitor is now in the process of arranging six-weekly weekend respite for Lester to give dad a break.'

REFLECTIVE TASK

Both Maryam and Frank are working inter-professionally and in a collaborative manner here.

- *What are the factors that are hindering effective multi-agency working in Maryam's situation?*

- *What are the factors that are promoting successful multi-agency working in Frank's setting?*

- *Note down your experience of communicating with other professionals, beyond your actual setting.*

- *What opportunities do you have to lead others in contributing to the work of a multi-professional team (S36)?*

In the past decade or so, there have been an unprecedented number of sweeping changes and reforms in services for children and families. As noted, there are further ambitious targets set for 2020. The roll-out of multi-professional practice is central to these reforms, though there remain mixed levels of confidence – from both the various professional bodies and the general public – about their effectiveness, while there is much to raise concern (UNICEF, 2007). As an EYP, you will have a key role to play in offering your wholehearted commitment to maximising your own skills and expertise in inter-professional collaboration and in leading others to use theirs to the full.

C H A P T E R   S U M M A R Y

In this chapter you have had an opportunity to reflect on the role of the practice. First, we considered the three elements involved in collabora families: partnership, continuity, and empowerment and educati challenges in working with families and the extent of their involvement learning particularly have been highlighted and you are reminded of allowing parents to retain choice in the pace and breadth of their involvement. In the second half of the chapter we have attempted to engage with some of the key issues relating to inter-professional communication and collaboration. Whilst integrated service provision and formalised multi-agency working may not be part of the EYP role for many of you, the importance of contributing your professional expertise, within a multi-professional context, in improving the outcomes for all children and their families has been emphasised.

Moving on

In the next and final chapter, we focus on the final EYP Standards (38 and 39) and the importance of the EYP role in demonstrating an active commitment to continuing professional development for her/himself and inspiring and leading colleagues to take responsibility for identifying and meeting their own professional development needs. The core theme will be that of a 'community of learners' committed to a process of lifelong learning, aspiring not only to establishing quality practice and provision but to continual reflection on and enhancement of this.

Self-assessment questions

Reflect back on the aspects of the EYP role covered in this chapter and then complete the following exercises.

1: Carry out a self-audit of skills in collaborative working with parents and families.

Aspect of practice	Personal strengths/ experience	Skills in/opportunities to lead practice and links with EYPS Standards	Issues for development
Partnership in children's learning and development			
Continuity and progression, including transitions			
Empowerment and educational opportunities for parents/families			
Modes of communication: • routine • written • oral • visual			

2: Carry out a SWOT analysis of those aspects of your current role which include inter-professional collaboration. Identify your Strengths, Opportunities, Weaknesses and Threats, particularly in your leadership role.

Stengths	**Opportunities**
Weaknesses	**Threats**

What conclusions can you draw from this analysis? Is there any action you can take to enhance the 'strengths' and 'opportunities' and to minimise the 'weaknesses' and 'threats'?

FURTHER READING

Langston, A. (2006) Why parents matter. In Abbott, L. and Langston, A. *Parents Matter.* Maidenhead: Open University Press.

Pen Green Team (2007) All about . . . working with parents. Available on EYFS CD-ROM: The Early Years Foundation Stage, file://D:/resources/downloads/2.2_a.pdf

Powell, J. (2007) Multi-agency development and issues of communication. In Nurse, A. (ed.) *The New Early Years Professional: Dilemmas and Debates.* London: David Fulton.

See also a helpful range of Fact Sheets produced by the CWDC to enhance your understanding of inter-professional collaboration, at www.cwdccouncil.org.uk and www.everychildmatters.gov.uk.

9 Professional development

CHAPTER OBJECTIVES

This final chapter offers the opportunity to define 'professionalism' as core to the EYP role and its application in the context of Early Years practice. We consider the importance of continuing professional development (CPD) for the EYP, especially in refining and re-defining understanding of 'leadership' of practice. We discuss how CPD is crucial to building and sustaining self-confidence in this role, particularly in nurturing the confidence and competence of others. The creation and maintenance of a constructive approach to self-evaluation within Early Years settings is outlined and the role of the EYP in leading and supporting others in self-critical practice is addressed. One important aspect of the EYP role lies in identifying and encouraging the EYPs of the future. Case studies and reflective tasks are offered to support these themes.

After reading this chapter you should be able to:
- understand the concept of 'professionalism' within Early Years practice;
- identify the importance of continuing professional development for the leader of practice;
- evaluate the EYP role in supporting the continuing professional development of colleagues;
- appraise critically your own strengths and areas for development in these areas;
- apply your understanding to the preparation of your evidence for EYP validation.

This chapter has a broad focus and can be applied to all the EYP Standards as you seek to apply your knowledge, understanding to all aspects of your practice. You might like to focus on Standards 1–6 and on Standards 38 and 39 in particular.

Introduction

The concept of a 'profession' is commonly of a group of people who work in a 'defined way' and for an 'explicit purpose' (Nurse, 2007: 2). In the last chapter, there was much reference to inter-*professional* collaboration and multi-*professional* working, and by this it was clear we were referring to different spheres of employment: health; social work; family support; law enforcement and – for ourselves – Early Years practice. Here we pause to consider what we mean by professionalism in the context of Early Years practice. The emergence of the status of Early Years Professional (CWDC, 2007c), by its very name and validation process, is indicative of a drive to introduce a new understanding of professionalism into Early Years practice (Brock, 2006).

What, then, do we mean by the professional dimension to the EYP role? A positive and creative attitude to continuing professional development and lifelong learning is a key feature of this. As a leader of practice, you also have the responsibility of demonstrating this to colleagues and encouraging each of them to map and evidence their own professional development.

The professional role

How might we describe professional identity? Anning et al. (2006: 7) suggest that it is forged by 'a particular knowledge base, set of values, training and standing in the community'. What does this have to say about the dimensions of your professional role as an EYP? The 'knowledge base' is wide-ranging but refers particularly to your skills and expertise in leading the EYFS; and the awareness of and implications for practice of your own personal 'value stance' were outlined in our discussion of the essential skills for your role in leading equality practice. The issue of your 'standing in the community' is much more complex. We have identified the historical legacy of a low-paid, predominantly female Early Years workforce which lacked a clearly defined career structure. Changes in public perception of the new professionalism within Early Years practice will not be swift and may take up to a generation to become rooted in public consciousness. But, within the Early Years sector, there is neither despair nor complacency. From personal experience, most of us are aware of the positive changes that have already taken place, particularly over the past decade or so, and the profound effect these are having on the quality of life and learning for children and their families. Equally, we are aware of how much more there is to do. Indeed, this blend of positive rigour might be said to define the professional approach required for the role of EYP.

> *For me EYPS is about raising the profile of children. Lots of people working in childcare have lots of knowledge in different areas but this set of standards brings it all together and I hope it will result in consistency where people recognise how important the early years are. We do really good work and this needs to be recognised.*
>
> (EYP quoted by Ridge, 2006)

Friedland (2007: 126) describes professionalism in the Early Years as a 'ball of knotted string'. She describes the particular 'knots' which need untying in order to untangle the ball and reach a clear definition. We have already touched on some of these but you might like to reflect again on their particular impact on your professional role: gender; the changing role of women in society; power and status; definitions of 'professionalism' in wider society; ethical dimensions; issues of leadership; policy drivers – nationally and locally; and pay structures.

The concept of 'professionalism' in general has been much questioned from a post-modern perspective where categorisation of different 'professions' is seen to offer too restricted a use of knowledge and power (Frost, cited in Anning et al., 2006). The move towards multi-professional collaboration, and approaches such as the *Common Core of Skills and Knowledge* (HM Government , 2005) for all those working with children and families, will necessitate a much more fluid and broader definition of pro-fessionalism.

However, there have been helpful attempts to define professionalism in the Early Years. Moyles (2001) discusses this in the context of two further dimensions which she cites as 'passion' and 'paradox'. Moyles' main argument is for 'Early Years' to be viewed as a serious academic discipline and respected professional career pathway in its own right. Some years on, we might feel not only that was she right but that this has become well embedded within academia. The introduction of the DfES Sure Start Sector Endorsed Foundation Degree Early Years in 2002 and the EYP role in 2006 offers encouraging evidence for this. From research in both the UK and internationally, Moyles (2001) found that many Early Years practitioners expressed a passionate, highly enthusiastic commit-ment to their task. However, it is this passion, coupled with the particular challenges of the sector (the 'paradoxes') which is perceived as compromising the rigour by which early educators approach their work and, thus, the professional integrity of the role. Moyles argues that this is not the case and affirms strongly the distinctive element of passion, concluding:

Passion for young children is part of the culture of practitioners. Passion must be allowed, both as a panacea for coping with challenging paradoxes and also for inspiring pro-fessionalism in those who work and play with the youngest members of our society. (Moyles, 2001: 93)

CASE STUDY

Leila, a room leader in a Children's Centre

'I am absolutely passionate about what I do. I can't think of a better job! But I also know I have an awesome responsibility in helping shape the early learning experiences of young children and of engaging in partnership with their families in this. It's also not just about me; it's about a team approach here. There are days when things go wrong; the children's behaviour is very challenging, parents complain, there are difficulties within the staff team and then there are action plans to implement. I think if I lost the enthusiasm for the role I couldn't do it.'

- *What links can you draw between 'passion' and 'professionalism' here?*

- *How does this impact on the EYP role, especially in role-modelling good practice? Think about what motivates you in your role and how you are demonstrating professionalism in it.*

Rodd (2006) describes one of the products of becoming professional as additional moral/ethical obligations and responsibilities to children, their families, colleagues, the community and the wider profession itself. In the UK there is no formalised code of ethics for Early Years practice such as that developed in Australia (Australian Early Childhood Association Inc., 1991). Whilst those with professional roles in Early Years settings might have a strong commitment to acting in the best interests of the children in their care, such a code of ethics would offer a 'valuable tool for guiding the complex decision-making faced in day to day work with young children and their families' (Rodd, 2006: 254). One of your tasks in preparing for EYP validation is to reflect on a critical incident in your own practice. No doubt there will be many from which you might choose, as your role is reactive as well as proactive. In addition to your role in planning and implementing change over time, you need to respond 'in the now' to situations that transpire and present themselves for immediate action. Many would agree that an accepted code of ethics for such times would create greater professional confidence.

> .'*Ethical dilemmas are situations that involve conflict between core values and difficult, even painful choices that result in less than satisfactory outcome.*'
>
> (Fleet and Clyde, cited in Rodd, 2006: 254)

Andrea, a childminder, describes her dilemma

'*Kenny, a two-year-old, was about to start in my setting and I feel I had prepared well for his transition from his home setting to mine. However, I was very dismayed that on his first day with me, his mum had packed in his bag some flash cards and asked me to make sure I spent about half an hour going over the words with him. From my own personal and professional perspective, I don't feel this is appropriate for Kenny (or any two-year-old) and yet I also feel strongly about working in partnership with parents.*'

REFLECTIVE TASK

- *What are Andrea's professional choices here?*

- *What will guide her in decision-making?*

- *How might an agreed code of ethics support her in this?*

- *What would you do and why in this situation?*

Anning and Edwards (2006: 51) describe professional identity in the EYP role as 'a way of being, seeing and responding', responsively and flexibly maximising the learning potential of every aspect of Early Years practice, particularly in building on the children's own ideas, preferences and interests (Carr, 2001). Your understanding of your own professionalism is a critical factor in determining how effectively you carry out the EYP role. In introducing EYPS, the CWDC (2007a) is seeking to recognise your role as a highly skilled practitioner who will lead practice in raising the quality of provision and act as agent of change in all sectors of Early Years practice.

Continuing professional development

Pivotal to maintaining a professional stance is your commitment to ongoing professional development. Nutbrown (1996) described the right of every child to a 'respectful educator'. If we are to maintain the professional stance outlined above, you have a responsibility to be the best you can be in all aspects of the EYP role. Recommendations for improving practice and supporting professional development are clearly included in Section 1 of the *Practice Guidance for the Early Years Foundation Stage* (DfES, 2007b: 5). EYP S33 stresses the important link between reflection and professional development; the more skilled you become in evaluating the effectiveness of your own practice, the more you will be able to identify opportunities to enhance and develop your own expertise and knowledge.

Anning and Edwards suggest that 'children learn to love learning through being with adults who also love to learn'. Indeed, they believe that the process of professional development for Early Years practitioners itself mirrors the early learning process. For children and educators alike, the dispositions for learning are of equal if not greater importance than the 'what?' and the 'how?' of learning. They describe the essential dispositions for the inquiring professional as developing:

- the capacity to see the educational potential in experiences shared with children;

- the capacity to respond to the demands they have identified as they work with children;

- dispositions for enquiry and learning;

- ways of seeing and being seen which draw on the professional expertise of Early Years practitioners.

(Anning and Edwards, 2006: 145)

These can be developed through reading, working with a critical friend, the professional appraisal process, attendance at in-service training (INSET) events, further accredited study and career development. Effective leadership requires commitment to both the 'acquisition and the dissemination of knowledge' (Waniginayake, 2006: xii).

REFLECTIVE TASK

Read the account by EYP Angela of her personal learning journey in Appendix one, and then consider the following questions.

- *How is Angela demonstrating her commitment to ongoing professional development?*

- *What does Angela's story tell you about the professional values she holds?*

- *Can you begin to map your own learning journey towards EYPS and clarify your own personal value stance towards your role?*

Much available literature focuses significantly on the role of the Early Years practitioner in action research (Abbott and Moylett, 1997; Anning and Edwards, 2006; Rodd, 2006; Bottle, 2007) and this is increasingly seen as a key component in professionalism and professional development. Rodd (2006: 213) describes this as a 'tool for narrowing the gap between research and practice that enhances professional learning and fosters reflective practice'. Indeed, strong links have been drawn between action research and quality improvement in the services provided for young children (Macnaughton et al., cited in Rodd, 2006). How, then, does action research sit with the EYP role?

Early Years practitioners in this country are not as confident about action research as their counterparts in other countries, where this aspect of practice is well embedded within the pedagogue role (Bottle, 2007). We have highlighted frequently that one of your tasks as an EYP is to make professional judgements about the children in your setting. Indeed, the first of the three generic skills identified for the EYP is: 'the ability to make decisions based on sound judgement' (CWDC, 2007b: 9) Sound professional judgements are based to a large extent on the systematic collection and recording of information and the thoughtful analysis of this information based on wider reading (Willan, 2004).

Much of the inherited knowledge and many of the traditional practices within Early Years are based on research evidence (Piaget, Vygotsky, Bruner etc.). You can read more about these in the child development literature such as Bee and Boyd (2006). Equally, few Early Years practitioners can be unaware of the international dimension of Early Years and how this, too, is influencing current practice, particularly the understanding of pedagogy emerging from Reggio Emilia (Abbott and Nutbrown, 2001) and the shape of the early childhood curriculum in New Zealand (New Zealand Ministry of Education, 1996). The influence and impact on contemporary Early Years provision of the early pioneers and major theorists and insights from other parts of the world cannot be overemphasised. However, as reflective EYPs, it is important to understand that no theory or framework can be imported 'whole' and imposed on a particular setting. We have clearly established the situational/contextual element of the EYP role and it is essential that you develop professional confidence in your own capacity to make judgements about the children and families in your setting, based on your own gathered evidence and wider reading.

Responsibilities for the professional development of colleagues

When asked how they encouraged the professional development of others, a group of EYPs offered the following.

REFLECTIVE TASK

Think about an issue/aspect of practice on which you have led change recently. Try to note down the ways in which you used any of the following to inform the way you led the change:

- *your own observations;*

- *reading;*

- *INSET;*

- *conversations with a critical friend.*

'I update and train staff on developments in Early Years, particularly on the use of ICT'

(Manager, private day nursery)

'I am currently implementing a supervision programme within my setting which also feeds into the individual training programme of others'

(Teacher, day nursery)

'I encourage others to attend training courses (and remind them as necessary). I buy and then lend books to colleagues which might be useful, for instance I recommend the ICAN materials which support language development'

(Childminder)

'All the nurseries completed a quality accreditation scheme with my support'

(Teacher, chain of private day nurseries)

In your lead role as an 'agent of change' (CWDC, 2007a: 1) you will mainly be working with colleagues. The task of supporting others in their professional development is varied and will indeed include many of the elements identified above. You have a clear role in updating and training on developments in Early Years practice, particularly relating to the delivery of the EYFS. You will support quality enhancement in the setting and recommend training events and reading materials to colleagues. Within your role as mentor, you may well have key responsibilities in practitioner appraisal processes.

REFLECTIVE TASK

Take a few moments now to think about your role in supporting the professional development of colleagues. Can you describe how you see this in one or two sentences – as the EYPs quoted above have done? Note down your answer. In what way do you feel you are demonstrating leadership of practice in this role?

Consider here how a manager in a day nursery responded to this task:

I recognise the importance of my own professional development especially when I am tired and enthusiasm for the role is flagging. Engaging in professional development for myself gives me a push and I know that it can only strengthen me as a professional and that I can then pass on my skills to others.

(Manager, full day care nursery)

In attending vigilantly to your own professional development and life-long learning journey you are transmitting powerful messages to colleagues and role-modelling effective practice. In your role as mentor to colleagues – which is integral to their professional development – you are engaging in *guided participation* (Rogoff, 1991, cited in Anning and Edwards, 2006). This is comparable to the child's experience of early learning in a safe and well-supported environment. One of your tasks in supporting the professional development of others is to empower and enable them to take their own learning forward by offering them a secure base from which to launch their professional development. You will best achieve this by actively encouraging them and listening to them as part of your role.

Drawing on their own research into professional development in the Early Years, Anning and Edwards (2006) conclude that guided participation is a critical factor. This is akin to the mentoring role where a more experienced practitioner supports a less experienced colleague by role-modelling appropriate actions and strategies. It also involves leading collaborative discussions on planning and reviewing change. You might support colleagues through joint collection and analysis of data, including sharing in any frameworks for data collection such as observation schedules. This will offer them a shared focus on the children's experience of learning and provision.

It was Dewey (1938) who first coined the concept of 'co-creating learning' in the school context. Rogoff (1991) developed this further, and the pedagogical principles of Reggio Emilia (Abbott and Nutbrown, 2001) and the work from the Pen Green Centre (Whalley, 2005b) root this firmly within the context of Early Years. Concepts such as 'communities of learners', with children, families and practitioners all 'co-creators in the learning process', will inspire you in the EYP role; you are encouraged to read more about the Pen Green Centre and the work of the Reggio Emilia pre-schools and, if you have the opportunity, to visit them as part of your own continuing professional development.

You have a key role in leading practice by contributing to such an ethos of 'community learning' in your own setting. Louis et al. (1996, cited in Anning and Edwards, 2006) identify five significant components for an effective learning community. We have touched on a number of these already but they are included again here as they offer you a further opportunity to reflect on these aspects of practice and how you integrate these into your EYP role:

- **a shared sense of purpose** – bearing in mind that this takes time to achieve;

- **a collective focus on children's learning** – the creation of contexts, plans and evaluative actions taken to support children's holistic development;

- **purposeful collaborative activity** – this includes not only the immediate team of practitioner in the setting but also parents, families and other professionals involved with the practice in the setting;

- **deprivatised activity** – all practices need to be visible and transparent to colleagues and parents (Reggio Emilia settings use the documentation of children's learning as a key tool in deprivatising [Edwards and Forman, 1993]);

- **reflective dialogue** – leading evaluative discussion of key aspects of practice but also actively encouraging the full participation of colleagues.

REFLECTIVE TASK

For this task, read the account of Pia, who has developed a shared approach to professional development in her own setting, in Appendix 2.

- *Can you identify ways in which Pia has helped create a 'community of learners' in her own setting? How has she included all the 'stakeholders' here?*

REFLECTIVE TASK CONTINUED

- Think about the three key factors that Pia identifies. How critical do you feel these to be in creating such a learning community?

- Are you able to identify more effective ways of encouraging the professional development of colleagues in your own setting?

Professional development in context

In work originally applied to school-based practitioners, Morant (1981, cited in Smith and Langston, 1999) identified four types of professional development needs, and this may be useful in helping you as EYP to decide the appropriate approach to supporting individual colleagues. There are **induction** needs for new staff members, especially those who are newly qualified. Then there are **extension** needs for those who are well-established and are open and responsive to fresh challenges and new ideas. Third, there are **refreshment** needs for those who are returning from a career gap or long-term absence or where a new initiative requires *all* practitioners to update their practice. Finally, there are **conversion** needs for those whose career paths might diversify. This fits well within our contemporary context of multi-agency partnerships.

In the EYP role, you are promoting autonomy within colleagues, encouraging them to identify their own professional development needs through a process of self-evaluation. The principles of reflective practice can be applied here as you role-model a self-evaluative/ appraisal approach to your own role and encourage colleagues to do the same. This will involve more than simply highlighting current strengths, areas for development in practice and any training needs; if effective, the process will also help colleagues to become more aware of their own value stance and to identify possible career plans.

REFLECTIVE TASK

- Are you able to identify ways in which you support colleagues in effective self-evaluation or appraisal?

- How might you use your reflections on this to build evidence for S38 and 39?

Identifying and encouraging future EYPs

We know that the Government vision is the creation of a 'world class workforce in the Early Years to improve outcomes for children' (CWDC, 2007c: 4). You have already played a crucial role in fulfilling this vision in your own personal journey towards EYPS. Once you have achieved this status, you will be identifying colleagues who may be ready to begin their own pathways towards EYPS. The overall rationale for a new understanding of 'professionalism' in the Early Years workforce is to improve workforce skills and develop a trained bank of graduate workers whose knowledge and competences will be key to effective delivery of EYFS provision. Your role in supporting and encouraging future leaders of practice is one you should embrace wholeheartedly.

C H A P T E R   S U M M A R Y

We have considered the gradual process towards a more professional understanding of Early Years practice and practitioners. We have identified some of the complexities in defining professionalism in the contemporary context of inter-agency working but, nonetheless, highlighted the key components of professionalism in the Early Years as a distinctive knowledge base, set of values, training pathway and status in the community. In supporting the professional development of others, one of the most effective strategies is that of the EYP role-modelling an enthusiastic commitment to her/his own continuing development. The creation of a community of learners is a goal to which all EYPs should aspire as children, families, practitioners and the wider community engage in effective collaboration for the benefit of all. Within such a community, not only will children's learning and development needs be met effectively but so will those of the practitioners. In such an environment, future EYPs can be nurtured successfully and the role of the leader of practice will be embedded within the children's workforce. Such leaders will be able to demonstrate:

- reflective and reflexive practice in their own roles and skills in decision-making;

- sound knowledge and understanding of Early Years pedagogy: the holistic needs of all children from birth to five and competence in planning, implementing and monitoring within the framework of the Early Years Foundation Stage framework (DfES, 2007a);

- strong values of the intrinsic worth of each child and all those in her/his world;

- the ability to role-model, lead and support others in high quality practice;

- the ability to define a vision for practice within a setting;

- competence as an agent of change.

Self-assessment questions

1: Your own professional development journey

What do you understand now about the professional dimension to your role as EYP?

Issue for continuing professional development:	Why is it an issue for you now?	How might you address this need?

2: Leading and supporting others in their professional development

Question:	How do you know? Evidence from practice	Area for development
1. What is your experience of leading and supporting the professional development of colleagues in your setting?		
2. What opportunities do you create for reflective dialogue, as part of your role as leader of practice?		
3. In what ways are you helping the creation of a 'community of learners' in your setting?		
4. How do you encourage staff to engage in a process of regular self-evaluation/appraisal of their practice?		
5. How do/might you identify potential future EYPs?		

FURTHER READING

Anning, A. and Edwards, A. (2006) Creating contexts for professional development. In *Promoting Children's Learning from Birth to Five: Developing the New Professional* (2nd edn). Maidenhead: Open University Press.

Friedland, R. (2007) Professionalism in the Early Years. In Wild, M. and Mitchell, H. (eds) *Early Childhood Studies: Reflective Reader.* Exeter: Learning Matters.

Appendix 1: Angela's professional journey

When I left school I completed my NNEB at college before holding positions in a range of settings: practitioner in private day nursery, nursery nurse in maintained nursery school (here I worked with an inspirational headteacher who had a profound impact on me in terms of children's creativity), supply work in Reception and Year 1 classes, pre-school leader of a 24-place setting.

When my daughter was born in 1996 I knew I wanted to stay at home with her but needed some income – so at this point became a registered childminder. I built up my reputation locally and really enjoyed building partnerships with a number of children and families. Reflecting on my early days of childminding I realise there were times, though, when I felt quite isolated.

Five years on, as a family, we relocated to a small rural farming village. I re-registered as a childminder but instantly found there did not seem to be the same need for a child-minding service within the village as there was a lot of extended family childcare provision. I minded two children on a very part-time basis but needed to find some other type of work for my own motivation and got a job-share position as leader of a local pre-school which I was able to combine with my childminding work.

Being a pre-school leader was a real challenge though very enjoyable. It was in carrying out the leadership role at pre-school that I became aware of the rapid changes within the Early Years sector. I considered carefully whether my NNEB qualification was going to be enough if I was going to stay long-term in the sector and began to make tentative enquiries about furthering my qualifications.

I learned of the opportunity offered through the Sector Endorsed Early Years Foundation Degree (SEFDEY) which I commenced in 2003. By 2004, a couple of other families had made enquiries about my childminding services and I realised that I was keen just to focus on this role so I gave up the post of pre-school leader. I strongly believe young children are best cared for in a home-to-home environment.

I found the SEFDEY hard work, especially in juggling all the other demands in my life, but I loved it and feel I learnt loads and was constantly growing in confidence. Initially when faced with presentations and assignments I didn't know how I would get through but my tutors and workplace mentor helped me greatly and I found myself enjoying being in control and being able to express to others my passionate belief in the importance of the Early Years. I had become involved with my local childminding group and began to cascade information to them.

In 2005, I applied for one of the Link Childminder positions in my area and was offered one of the posts. My earlier experience of isolation influences me very strongly in this role as I feel the early days of registration can be lonely and a daunting role for new child-minders.

In 2006, I graduated from the SEFDEY with distinction and wanted to explore appropriate ways of continuing to study and reflect on my practice. I learned of the opportunity through my local university of an Extended Foundation Degree opportunity which offered me a 'top-up' of 60 credits at level 6. This was flexibly delivered and the modules offered excellent opportunity for further reflection on key aspects of Early Years practice and provision.

At the end of 2007 I heard that my local authority was recruiting tutors to deliver a new qualification for registered childminders. I was appointed and am thoroughly enjoying this role which I combine with my continued role as a childminder myself. The learners are very responsive and I adopt an interactive approach because as a part-time childminder myself, I am able to relate to real-life childminding situations. It has been a challenge working with three different stakeholders in the organisation of the course, but I have ensured that my presentation and delivery have been of a high quality.

I am now thinking 'what next?' I am hoping to prepare for EYPS validation and embark on further study to honours degree level. I would like to start the National Childminding Association Quality Assurance Scheme and continue to develop my tutoring role.

Ultimately, I would love to apply for one of the Area Childminding Support Officer posts but there are currently only four in the county! I certainly feel I have considerable know-ledge and experience in the field of childminding and home-based services and want to continue to put these to good use. I genuinely love being with the children and want to continue this as part of my role.

Appendix 2: Pia is the leader of a pre-school playgroup and describes her 'learning community'

I qualified as a teacher in Sweden but when I moved to this country it was not possible to continue in this role without further (costly) training. At that point, I started working in a playgroup, as a waitress and as a railway conductor, while deciding what to do with my future. As it turned out I had my two children at that point and this led me, a little later, to join another playgroup, becoming treasurer and later joining the staff team.

As this proves, I hadn't until recently planned my professional development at all, but was instead driven by a wish to learn as much as I could about the field I'm working in and related issues – i.e. children's learning and development, parental involvement etc. It was thus that I 'slid into' studying for a certificate in management. Part of this study entailed creating a professional development plan and it soon became apparent how useful this is; if nothing else, it highlights how much I actually do to keep up-to-date with current issues in my field.

I am currently working as a play leader in a small setting: a parent-managed pre-school playgroup, registered for 30 children. There is no traditionally carved career path, with opportunities for 'promotion' within the setting for me. I find that most of the professional development I undertake, and want to undertake, is to improve my practice in my current role. I am currently on the path of achieving EYPS and am not yet sure what other opportunities and challenges this might open up for me.

As the 'Learning for Life' and 'Every Child/Parent Matters' agendas further permeate the social structure, I sense that all Early Years settings are/will be working more and more with (or at least with the ideal of) parents as partners, which is the main reason I've worked within the pre-school movement. How then do I encourage others? When I reflect on this, I believe there are three key factors:

Vision: I encourage colleagues to commit to their own continuing professional development through my vision. I am aware that my formative years in Sweden have helped to shape my personal stance that everyone has equal rights to a fulfilling life, and one of the main reasons I've remained with the pre-school setting is that not only have I the privilege of learning with the children, I also do the same with their mums and dads and wider families. Being a 'new' parent is one of the greatest and at times hardest things and we see one of our important roles as building our setting's 'community' into a supportive network; we are stronger together. I believe that we are all learners (adults as well as children) and I want us to build 'a learning community'. This often leads to parents being encouraged to begin/continue studying as they continue or change career into a child-related one. Involvement on our committee may also lead to increased self-confidence and so to other study. Within our staff team, seven out of eleven of us started as parents in the setting, some with, but most without, any related qualifications. We now have six members of staff, myself included, who are studying – from level 1 right up to honours degree level and working towards EYPS.

Time: I believe that the committee's and my commitment to 'non-contact' time has a big part to play in the staff team development. We are paid to meet once a week, discussing not only the children's learning and planning for this, but also our own – short courses we have been on, reading materials, qualification studies, it all gets discussed. The support is there, not only from me, but from the whole team. This doesn't mean that we always agree – on the contrary – but then that is when you get a real chance to assess your own viewpoint and also to learn from each other. These meetings also offer time to discuss our learning ethos and the views of the children. We also have three in-house training sessions a year – looking at different issues, such as 'assessment and observation – the adult's role', 'planning', etc. Sometimes I decide on content, sometimes another staff member asks for a certain issue to be covered.

Leadership: I asked my staff individually about why they thought so many of us were studying at the moment and my role in this. Some mentioned that I acted as inspiration by studying myself. The reassurance that support was there helped, according to some, along with opportunities to share, discuss (and put into practice) things learnt. Some staff highlighted that how things were learnt was important. One member of staff said it helped to break down her resistance to further learning, when she realised that if others could do it, so could she. Nearly all staff also mentioned that the practical support I gave was important, advising on the different routes to qualifications. The most important factor that all the staff mentioned, however, was help with the financial side; me knowing the ins-and-outs of bursaries and other grants means that it's affordable for them – I have also negotiated with the committee, so that the setting now funds staff fully to achieve a Level 2 qualification, on the proviso that they stay with us for two years afterwards.

I have always seen as one aspect of my role the bringing into focus (for all adults – parents as well as staff) the great privilege of being allowed to, every day, share and be part of the miracle of the 'EUREKA-moments', the wide-eyed wonder and the awe of young learning – it's contagious and inspiring. I believe that taking time to discuss these moments every day not only celebrates each child's learning, but also encourages adults towards learning themselves – it's fun to learn!

References

Abbott, L. and Moylett, H. (1997) *Working with the Under-3s: Training and Professional Development*. Buckingham: Open University Press.

Abbott, L. and Nutbrown, C. (2001) *Experiencing Reggio Emilia: Implications for Pre-School Provision*. Buckingham: Open University Press.

Alliance for Inclusive Education (1990) Principles, available at http://www.allfie.org.uk/pages06/about/index.html (accessed 19 November 2007).

Anning, A. and Edwards, A. (2006) *Promoting Children's Learning from Birth to Five: Developing the New Early Years Professional*. Maidenhead: Open University Press.

Anning, A., Cottrell, D., Frost, N., Green, J. and Robinson, M. (2006) *Developing Multiprofessional Teamwork for Integrated Children's Services*. Maidenhead: Open University Press.

Antoniou, L. (2005) Inclusion in early years settings. *Under Five*, April 2005: 12–13.

Appleton, P. L. and Minchom, P. E. (1991) Models of parent partnership and child development centres. *Child: Care, Health and Development*, 17: 27–8.

Armstrong, M. (1994) *How to be an Even Better Manager*. London: Kogan Page.

Athey, C. (2007) *Extending Thought in Young Children: A Parent-Teacher Partnership* (2nd edn). London: Paul Chapman.

Atkinson, M., Wilkin, A., Stott, A., Doherty, P. and Kinder, K. (2002) *Multi-Agency Working: A Detailed Study*. Slough: National Foundation for Educational Research.

Aubrey, C. (2007) *Leading and Managing in the Early Years*. London: Sage.

Australia Early Childhood Association Inc. (1991) Australian Early Childhood Association Code of Ethics. *Australian Journal of Early Childhood*, 16 (1): 3–6.

Ball, C. (1994) *Start Right: The Importance of Early Learning*. London: Royal Society for the Encouragement of the Arts, Manufacturing and Commerce.

Bandura, A. (1977) *Social Learning Theory*. London: Prentice Hall.

Barnett, J. (2008) Mentoring, boundaries and multiple relationships: opportunities and challenges. *Mentoring and Tutoring: Partnership in Learning*, 16 (1), 3–16.

Bass, B. M. (1985) *Leadership and Performance Beyond Expectation*. New York: Free Press.

Bass, B. M. and Stodgill, R. M. (1990) *Handbook of Leadership: Theory, Research and Managerial Applications*. New York: Free Press.

Bax, M. (2001) Endeavours of Parents, Editorial in *Developmental Medicine and Child Neurology*, 43: 291.

Bee, H. and Boyd, D. (2006) *The Developing Child*. London: Pearson Education.

Belbin, M. (1993) *Team Roles at Work*. Cambridge: Belbin Associates.

Bennis, W. (1998) *On Becoming a Leader*. London: Arrow.

Bertram, T. and Pascal, C. (2002) *Early Years Education: An International Perspective*. London: QCA.

Blake, R. and Mouton, J. (1964) *The Managerial Grid: The Key to Leadership Excellence*. Houston: Gulf Publishing Co.

Bloom, P. J. (1997) Navigating the rapids: directors reflect on their career and professional development. *Young Children*, 52 (7): 32–8.

Bloom, P. J.(2000) How do we define director competence? *Childcare Information Exchange*, 138: 13–18.

Boddy, J., Cameron, C., Moss, P., Mooney, A., Petrie, P. and Statham, J. (2005) *Introducing Pedagogy into the Children's Workforce: Children's Workforce Strategy – A Response to the Consultation*. London: Thomas Coram Research Unit/Institute of Education, University of London.

Bolman, L. G. and Deal, T. E. (1997) *Reframing Organizations. Artistry, Choice and Leadership* (2nd edn). San Francisco: Jossey-Bass.

Bottery, M. (1990) *The Morality of the School*. London: Cassell.

Bottle, G. (2007) Research in the Early Years. In Nurse, A. (ed.) *The New Early Years Professional: Dilemmas and Debates*. London: David Fulton.

British Educational Research Association Early Years Special Interest Group (2003) *Pedagogy, Curriculum, Adult Roles, Training and Professionalism*. London: BERA.

Brock, A. (2006) Dimensions of early years professionalism – attitudes versus competences? Reflection Paper for Training Advancement and Cooperation in Teaching Young Children (TACTYC), available at http://www.tactyc.org.uk/pdfs/Reflection_brock.pdf (accessed: 30 November 2007).

Bronfenbrenner, U. (1979) *The Ecology of Human Development*. Cambridge, MA: Harvard University Press.

Brookfield, S. D. (1995) *Becoming a Critically Reflective Teacher*. San Francisco: Jossey-Bass.

Bruce, T., Whalley, M., Mairs, K., Arnold, C. and the Centre Team (1997) Case Study Two: a family centre. In Pascal, C. and Bertram, T. *Effective Early Learning: Case Studies in Improvement (Zero to Eight Series)*. London: Paul Chapman.

Bruce, T. (2004) *Developing Learning in Early Childhood*. London: Paul Chapman.

Bryman, A. (1986) *Charisma and Leadership in Organisations*. London: Routledge and Kegan Paul.

Bubb, S. (2005) *Helping Teachers Develop*. London: Paul Chapman.

Burns, J. M. (1978) *Leadership*. New York: HarperCollins.

Burton, G. and Dimbleby, R. (1988) *Teaching Communication*. London: Routledge.

Bush, T. and Middlewood, D. (2005) *Leading and Managing People in Education*. London: Sage.

Bruce, T. (2004) *Developing Learning in Early Childhood*. London: Paul Chapman.

Callan, S. (2006) What is mentoring? In Robbins, A. (ed.) *Mentoring in the Early Years*. London: Paul Chapman.

Callan, S. and Copp, E. (2006) The mentor as the one in the middle. In Robbins, A. (ed.) *Mentoring in the Early Years*. London: Paul Chapman.

Carr, M. (2001) *Assessment in Early Childhood Settings: Learning Stories*. London: Sage/Paul Chapman.

Chakraborty, D. (2003) Leadership in the East and West: a few examples. *Journal of Human Values*, 9; 29–52.

Children's Workforce Development Council (CWDC) (2005) *Children's Workforce Strategy: A Consultation*. London: CWDC.

CWDC (2007a) *Guidance to the Standards for the Award of Early Years Professional Status*. London: CWDC.

CWDC (2007b) *Early Years Professional Status: Candidates' Handbook*. London: CWDC.

CWDC (2007c) *Early Years Professional Status: Prospectus*. London: CWDC.

CWDC) (2007d) Integrated working, available at www.cwdccouncil.org.uk/projects/integrated working.htm (accessed 18 November 2007).

CWDC (2007e) The Lead Professional: fact sheet, available at http://www.everychildmatters.gov. uk/_files/B4262FC32B9195966529242F2FC2C9CA.pdf (accessed 18 November 2007).

CWDC (2007f) Common Assessment Framework: fact sheet, available at http://www.everychild matters.gov.uk/_files/2F072A048CAB38561EA2E23BB5F74F62.pdf (accessed 18 November 2007).

Clark, K. E. and Clark, M. B. (eds) (1990). *Measures of Leadership*. Greensboro, NC: Center for Creative Leadership.

Connolly, P. (2004) *Boys and Schooling in the Early Years*. London: RoutledgeFalmer.

Connor, M. and Pokora, J. (2007) *Coaching and Mentoring at Work: Developing Effective Practice*. Maidenhead: Open University Press.

Costa, A. and Kallick, B. (1993) Through the lens of a critical friend. *Educational Leadership*, 51 (2), 49–51.

Covey, S. R. (1989) *The Seven Habits of Highly Effective People*. Boston, MA: Harvard Business School Press.

Cox, E. (1996) *Leading Women: Tactics for Making the Difference*. Sydney: Random House.

Cuban, L. (1988) *The Managerial Imperative and the Practice of Leadership in Schools*. Albany, NY: State University of New York.

CUREE (2005) The National Framework for Mentoring and Coaching, available at http://www. curee-paccts.com/dynamic/curee75.jsp.

Daly, M. Byers, E. and Taylor, W. (2004) *Early Years Management in Practice*. London: Heinemann.

Dana, N. F. and Yendol-Hoppey, D. (2005) Becoming an early childhood teacher leader and an advocate for social justice: a phenomenological interview study. *Journal of Early Childhood Teacher Education*, 26: 191–206.

David, T., Goouch, K., Powell, S. and Abbott, L. (2003) *Birth to Three Matters: A Review of the Literature*. London: DfES Publications.

Department for Children, Schools and Families (DCSF) (2007a) *Raising Standards – Improving Outcomes*. London: HMSO.

DCSF (2007b) *Children's Plan – Building Brighter Futures*. Norwich: HMSO.

DCSF (2007c) Principles into Practice Cards *The Early Years Foundation Stage*. Nottingham: DCSF.

DCSF (2008a) *Statutory Framework for the Early Years Foundation Stage*. Nottingham: DCSF.

DCSF (2008b) *Practice Guidance for the Early Years Foundation Stage*. Nottingham: DCSF.

DCSF (2008c) Effective Practice: Inclusive Practice. Resource on CD-Rom. *The Early Years Foundation Stage*. Nottingham: DCSF.

DCSF (2008d) Resource on CD-Rom. *The Early Years Foundation Stage*. Nottingham: DCSF.

Department for Education and Employment (DFEE) (2000) *Curriculum Guidance for the Foundation Stage*. London: Qualifications and Curriculum Authority (QCA).

Department of Education and Science (DES) (1990) *Starting with Quality: Report of the Committee of Inquiry into the Quality of Educational Experience Offered to Three and Four Year Olds* (Rumbold report). London: DES/HMSO.

Department for Education and Skills (DfES) (2001) *National Standards for Day Care and Childminding*. London: DfES.

DfES (2002) *Birth to Three Matters: A Framework for Supporting Children in Their Earliest Years*. London: DfES.

DfES (2003) *Every Child Matters* (Green Paper). London: HMSO.

DfES (2004a) *Every Child Matters: Change for Children*. Nottingham: DfES.

DfES (2004b) *Statutory Guidance on Making Arrangements to Safeguard and Promote the Welfare of Children under section 11 of the Children Act 2004; Every Child Matters: Change for Children*. Nottingham: DfES.

DfES (2006a) *Children's Workforce Strategy: The Government's Response to the Consultation*. Nottingham: DfES.

DfES (2006b) *Championing Children: A Shared Set of Skills, Knowledge and Behaviours for Those Leading and Managing Integrated Children's Services*. Nottingham: DfES.

DfES and Price Waterhouse Coopers (2007) *Independent Study of School Leadership*. Nottingham: DfES.

DfES/Sure Start (2007) *National Standards for Leaders of Sure Start Children's Centres*. Nottingham: DfES.

Dewey, J. (1933) *How We Think: A Restatement of the Relation of Reflective Thinking in the Educative Process*. Chicago: Henry Regnery.

Dewey, J. (1938) *Experience and Education*. New York: Simon and Schuster.

Dickins, M. (2002) All About . . . Anti-Discriminatory Practice. *Nursery World*, 3: 15–22.

Donaldson, M. (1978) *Children's Minds*. London: Fontana Press.

Doyle, M. E. and Smith, M. K. (1999) *Born and Bred? Leadership, heart and Informal Education*. London: YMCA George Williams College/The Rank Foundation.

Draper, L. and Duffy, B. (2006) Working with parents. In Pugh, G. and Duffy, B. (eds) *Contemporary Issues in the Early Years* (4th edn). London: Sage.

Dryden, W. and Constantinou, D. (2004) *Assertiveness Step By Step*. London: Sheldon Press.

Duck, J. D. (2001) *The Change Monster: The Human Forces that Fuel or Foil Corporate Transformation and Change*. New York: Crown Business.

Dwiveldi, K. N. (1996) Race and the child's perspective. In Davie, R., Upton, G. and Varma, V. (eds) *The Voice of the Child: A Handbook for Professionals*. London: Falmer Press.

Dyer, W. (1987) *Team Building* (2nd edn). Reading, MA: Addison-Wesley.

Ebbeck, M. and Waniganayake, M. (2003) *Early Childhood Professionals Leading Today and Tomorrow*. Sydney: Maclennan and Petty Ltd.

Edgington, M. (2004) *The Foundation Stage Teacher in Action* (3rd edn). London: Paul Chapman.

Edwards, A. (2000) Research and practice: is there a dialogue? In Penn, H. (ed.) *Early Childhood Services. Theory, Policy and Practice*. Buckingham: Open University Press.

Edwards, C. P. and Forman, G.E. (eds.) (1993) *The Hundred Languages of Children: Reggio Emilia Approach to Early Childhood*. Norwood, New Jersey: Ablex Publishing Inc.

Elfer, P, Goldschmied, E and Selleck, D. (2003) *Key Persons in the Nursery: building Relationships for Quality Provision* London: David Fulton.

Fiedler, F. E. and Garcia, J. E. (1987) *New Approaches to Effective Leadership*. New York: John Wiley.

Fisher, J. (2008) *Starting from the Child: Teaching and Learning in the Foundation Stage* (3rd edn). Maidenhead: Open University Press.

Fowler, K. (2005) Mind Tools on Active Listening, available at http://www.mindtools.com/CommSkll/Mind%20Tools%20Listening.pdf (accessed 23 November 2007).

Friedland, R. (2007) Professionalism in the early years. In Wild, M. and Mitchell, H. (eds) *Early Childhood Studies: Reflective Reader*. Exeter: Learning Matters.

Garbarino, J. with Abramowitz, R. H. (1992) *Children and Families in the Social Environment*. Berlin: Aldine de Gruyter.

Gardner, H. (1983) *Frames of Mind: Theories of Multiple Intelligences*. New York: Basic Books.

Gardner, J. (1989) *On Leadership*. New York: Free Press.

Garvey, B. (1999) Mentoring and the changing paradigm. *Mentoring and Tutoring*, 7 (1): 41–54.

Garvey, B. and Alred, G. (2000) Educating mentors. *Mentoring and Tutoring*, 8 (2): 113–26.

Gerhardt, S. (2004) *Why Love Matters*. Hove: Brunner-Routledge.

Ghaye, A. and Ghaye, K. (1998) *Teaching and Learning through Critical Reflective Practice*. London: David Fulton.

Gillen, T. (1995) *Positive Influencing Skills*. London: Chartered Institute of Personnel Development.

Glauert, E., Heal, C. and Cook, J. (2007) Knowledge and understanding of the world. In Riley, J. (ed.) *Learning in the Early Years* (2nd edn). London: Sage.

Goldschmied, E. and Jackson, S. (2004) *People Under Three: Young Children in Day Care* (2nd edn). London: Routledge.

Goleman, D. (1996) *Emotional Intelligence: Why It Can Matter More than IQ*. London: Bloomsbury.

Hawkey, K. (2006) Emotional intelligence and mentoring in pre-service teacher education: a literature review. *Mentoring and Tutoring*, 14 (2): 137–47.

Hall, V. (1996) *Dancing on the Ceiling*. London: Paul Chapman.

Hallet, E. (2004) The reflective practitioner. In Macleod-Brudenell, I. (ed.) *Advanced Care and Education Level 4 and 5*. Oxford: Heinemann Educational.

Harris, A., Day, C. and Hadfield, M. (2003) Teachers' perspectives on effective school leadership. *Teachers and Teaching: Theory and Practice*, 9 (1): 67–77.

Hatherley, A. and Lee, W. (2003) Voices of early childhood leadership. *New Zealand Journal of Educational Leadership*, 18: 91–100.

Hayden, J. (1997) Directors of early childhood services: experience, preparedness and selection. *Australian Research in Early Childhood*, 1 (1): 49–67.

Heifetz, R. A. (1994) *Leadership Without Easy Answers*. Cambridge, MA: Belknap Press.

Hersey, P. and Blanchard, K. H. (1977) *The Management of Organizational Behaviour*. Upper Saddle River, NJ: Prentice Hall.

Hirsch, D. (2007) *Chicken and Egg: Child Poverty and Educational Inequalities*. Child Poverty Action Group Briefing Paper, London: CPAG.

HM Government (2005) *Common Core of Skills and Knowledge for the Children's Workforce*. Nottingham: DfES.

HM Treasury (2004) *Choice for Parents, the Best Start for Children: A Ten Year Strategy for Childcare*. London: Stationery Office.

Home Office (2003) *The Victoria Climbié Inquiry: Report of an Inquiry by Lord Laming*. Norwich: Her Majesty's Stationery Office.

Horne, M. and Stedman Jones, D. (2001) *Leadership: The Challenge for All?* London: Institute of Management.

Hujala, E. (2004) Dimensions of leadership in the childcare context. *Scandinavian Journal of Educational Research*, 48 (1): 53–71.

Isaksen, S. and Tidd, J.(2006) *Meeting the Innovation Challenge*. Chichester: John Wiley and Sons.

Jackson, L. (2005) Who are you calling a pedagogue? *Guardian Unlimited* (18 May), available at http://www.guardian.co.uk/society/2005/may/18/socialcare.childrensservices (accessed 15 April 2008).

Jones, C. (2004) *Supporting Inclusion in the Early Years*. Maidenhead: Open University Press.

Kagan, S. L. and Hallmark, L. G. (2001) Cultivating leadership in early care and education. *Child Care Information Exchange*, 140: 7–10.

Karpf, A. (2007) Forget phonics – that's for teachers. Parents have fun with your kids. *The Guardian Family Supplement* (3 November), available at http://lifeandhealth.guardian.co.uk/family/story/0,,2216141,00.html (accessed 15 April 2008).

Kunesh, L. G. and Farley, J. (1993) *Collaboration: The Prerequisite for School Readiness and Success*. Arlington, VA: ERIC.

Lancaster, P. (2006) Listening to young children: respecting the voice of the child. In Pugh, G. and Duffy, B. (eds) *Contemporary Issues in the Early Years* (4th edn). London: Sage.

Langston, A. (2006) Why parents matter. In Abbott, L. and Langston, A. (eds) *Parents Matter: Supporting the Birth to Three Framework*. Maidenhead: Open University Press.

Langston, A. and Abbott, L. (2007) *Playing to Learn: Developing High Quality Experiences for Babies and Toddlers*. Maidenhead: Open University Press.

Lave, J. and Wenger, E. (1991) *Situated Learning: Legitimate Peripheral Participation*. Cambridge: Cambridge University Press.

Law, S. and Glover, D. (2000) *Educational Leadership and Learning: Practice, Policy and Research*. Buckingham: Open University Press.

Leeson, C. (2004) In praise of reflective practice. In Willan, J., Parker-Rees, R. and Savage, J. *Early Childhood Studies*. Exeter: Learning Matters.

Levy, R. (2007) A reading list to support continuing professional development. In Punter, A. (ed.) *Mentor Development for Teacher Training: A Scenario-Based Approach*. Hatfield: University of Hertfordshire Press.

Lindon, J. (2006) *Equality in Early Childhood: Linking Theory and Practice*. London: Hodder Arnold.

Louis, K. S. S., Marks, H. and Kruse, S. (1996) Teachers' professional communities in restructuring schools. *American Educational Research Journal*, 33 (4): 757–98.

Mann, R. D. (1959) A review of the relationship between personality and performance in small groups. *Psychological Bulletin*, 66 (4): 241–70.

Manning-Morton, J. and Thorp, M. (2003) *Key Times for Play*. Maidenhead: Open University Press.

Manning-Morton, J. and Thorp, M. (2006) *Key Times: A Framework for Developing High Quality Provision for Children from Birth to Three*. Maidenhead: Open University Press.

Marshall, J. (1994) Revisioning organisations by developing female values. In Boot, J., Lawrence, J. and Morris, J. (eds) *Managing the Unknown by Creating New Futures*. London: McGraw-Hill.

van Maurik, J. (2001) *Writers on Leadership*. London: Penguin.

McAuliffe, A., Linsey, A. and Fowler, J. (2006) *Childcare Act 2006: The Essential Guide*. NFER and NCB.

McCauley, C. D., Moxley, R. and van Velsor, E. (eds) (1998) *The Centre for Creative Leadership Handbook of Leadership Development*. San Francisco: Jossey-Bass.

McGregor, D. (1970) *The Human Side of Enterprise*. New York: McGraw-Hill.

Megginson, D., Clutterbuck, D., Garvey, G., Stokes, P. and Garrett-Harris, R. (2006) *Mentoring in Action: A Practical Guide* (2nd edn). London: Kogan Page.

Millar, F. (2008) How best to support parents will be key. *The Guardian Education Supplement* (15 January), available at http://education.guardian.co.uk/egweekly/story/0,,2240620,00.html (accessed 15 April 2008).

Mitchell, A. and Serranen, P. (2000) *Leadership for Change in the Primary Grades to Improve Student Achievement: A Report on the Success for All Children's Principals Academy*. Clayton, MO: Danforth Foundation.

Mitchell, H. (2007) The role of policymakers: rights and responsibilities. In Wild, M. and Mitchell, H. *Childhood Studies Reflective Reader*. Exeter: Learning Matters.

Morant, R. (1981) *In Service Education within the School*. London: Unwin.

Moss, P. and Petrie, P. (2002) *From Children's Services to Children's Spaces*. London: Taylor and Francis.

Moyles, J. (2001) Passion, paradox and professionalism in Early Years education. *Early Years*, 21 (2): 81–95.

Moyles, J. (ed.) (2005) *The Excellence of Play* (2nd edn). Maidenhead: Open University Press.

Moyles, J. (2006) *Effective Leadership and Management in the Early Years*. Maidenhead: Open University Press.

Moyles, J., Adams, S. and Musgrove, A. (2002) *SPEEL: The Study of Pedagogical Effectiveness in Early Learning*. Research Report 363, London: DfES.

Moylett, H. and Djemli, P. (2005) Practitioners matter. In Abbott, L. and Langston, A. (eds) *Birth to Three Matters*. Maidenhead: Open University Press.

Muijs, D., Aubrey, C., Harris, A. and Briggs, M. (2004) How do they manage? A review of the research in early childhood. *Journal of Early Childhood Research*, 2: 157, available at http://ecr.sagepub.com/cgi/content/abstreact/2/2/157 (accessed 19 October 2007). .

Murray, J. (2006) Designing and implementing a mentoring scheme: University of Worcester Sure Start-recognised sector-endorsed Foundation Degree in Early Years. In Robbins, A. (ed.) *Mentoring in the Early Years*. London: Paul Chapman.

Neugabauer, B. and Neugabauer, R. (eds) (1998) *The Art of Leadership: Managing Early Childhood Organisations* (vol. 2). Perth, Australia: Childcare Information Exchange.

New Zealand Ministry of Education (1996) *Te Wh_riki: Early Childhood Curriculum*. Wellington, NZ: Ministry of Education.

Noone, M. (1996) *Mediation*. London: Cavendish.

Nurse, A. (ed.) (2007) *The New Early Years Professional: Dilemmas and Debates*. London: David Fulton.

Nutbrown, C. (1996) *Respectful Educators – Capable Learners: Children's Rights and Early Education*. London: Paul Chapman.

Nutbrown, C. (2006) *Threads of Thinking: Young Children Learning and the Role of Early Education* (3rd edn). London: Sage.

Nutbrown, C. and Clough, P. (2006) *Inclusion in the Early Years*. London: Sage.

Office for Standards in Education (Ofsted) (2007) *The Foundation Stage: A Survey of 144*. London: Ofsted.

Office for Standards in Education (Ofsted) (2008) How we inspect, available at http://www.ofsted. gov.uk/portal/site/Internet/menuitem.455968b0530071c4828a0d8308c08a0c/?vgnextoid=defa 8487a73dc010VgnVCM1000003507640aRCRD.

Owen, S. (2006) Training and workforce issues in the Early Years. In Pugh, G. and Duffy, B. (eds) *Contemporary Issues in the Early Years* (4th edn). London: Sage.

Payler, J. (2005) Opening and closing interactive spaces: early years pedagogy and four year old children's contributions to it in two English settings. Conference Paper for British Educational Research Association Annual Conference, University of Glamorgan, 14–17 September 2005.

Pen Green Team (2007) All about . . . Working with Parents. Available on EYFS CD-ROM: The Early Years Foundation Stage, file://D:/resources/downloads/2.2_a.pdf.

Pound, L. (2005) Management, leadership and teamwork. In Dryden, L., Forbes, R., Mukherji, P., Pound, L., Chawla-Duggan, R., Joshi, U., Menon, C. and Trodd, L. *Essential Early Years*. London: Hodder Arnold.

Powell, J. (2005) Anti-discriminatory practice matters. In Abbott, L. and Langston, A. (eds) *Birth to Three Matters*. Maidenhead: Open University Press.

Powell, J. (2007) Multi-agency development and issues of communication. In Nurse, A. (ed.) *The New Early Years Professional: Dilemmas and Debates* London: David Fulton.

Pugh, G. (2006) The policy agenda for early childhood services. In Pugh, G. and Duffy, B. *Contemporary Issues in the Early Years* (4th edn). London: Sage.

Ramey, S. L., Ramey, C. T., Philips, M. M., Lanzi, R. G., Brezausek, C., Katholi, C. R., Snyders, S. and Lawrence, F. L. (2000) *Head Start Children's Entry into Public School: A Report on the National Head Start/Public School Early Childhood Transition Study*. Birmingham, AL: Curtan International Research Centre.

Ranson , R., Halpin, D., Nixon, J. and Seddon, T. (2004) Editorial. *London Review of Education*, 2 (3): 163–9. In Petrie, P. (2005) Extending pedagogy. *Journal of Education for Teaching*, 31 (4): 293–6.

Reed, M. (2008) Professional development through reflective practice. In Paige-Smith, A. and Craft, A. (eds) *Developing Reflective Practice in the Early Years*. Maidenhead: Open University Press.

Rhodes, C., Stokes, M. and Hampton, G. (2004) *A Practical Guide to Mentoring, Coaching and Peer-Networking: Teacher Professional Development in Schools and Colleges*. London: RoutledgeFalmer.

Ridge, M. (2006) The new professionals. *The Guardian* (11 July).

Robbins, A. (ed.) (2006) *Mentoring in the Early Years*. London: Sage.

Roberts, R. (2006) *Self-Esteem and Early Learning: Key People from Birth to School* (3rd edn). London: Paul Chapman.

Rodd, J. (1996) Towards a typology of leadership for the early childhood professional of the twenty-first century. *Early Childhood Development and Care*, 120: 119–26.

Rodd, J. (1997) Learning to be leaders: perceptions of early childhood professionals about leadership roles and responsibilities. *Early Years*, 18 (1): 40–46.

Rodd, J. (1998) *Leadership in Early Childhood: The Pathway to Professionalism* (2nd edn). Sydney: Allen and Unwin.

Rodd, J. (1999) *Leadership in Early Childhood* (1st edn). Buckingham: Open University Press.

Rodd, J. (2006) *Leadership in Early Childhood* (3rd edn). Maidenhead: Open University Press.

Rogers, C. (1961) *On Becoming a Person*. Boston, MA: Houghton Mifflin.

Rogoff, B. (1991) Social interaction as apprenticeship in thinking: guided participation in spatial planning. In Resnick, L., Levine, J. and Teasley, S. (eds) *Perspectives on Socially Shared Cognition*. Washington DC: APA.

Rosener, J. B. (1997). Sexual static. In Grint, K. (ed.) *Leadership:. Classical, Contemporary and Critical Approaches*. Oxford: Oxford University Press.

Sadler, P. (1997) *Leadership*. London: Kogan Page.

Samaras, A. (2002) *Self-Study for Teacher Educators*. New York: Peter Lang.

Savage, J. and Leeson, C. (2007) Leadership in early childhood settings. In Willan, J., Parker-Rees, R. and Savage, J. (eds) *Early Childhood Studies* (2nd edn). Exeter: Learning Matters.

Schön, D. (1983) *The Reflective Practitioner*. New York: Basic Books.

Schrag, L., Nelson, E. and Siminowsky, T. (1985) Helping employees cope with change. *Child Care Information Exchange* (September): 3–6.

Senge, P. M. (1994) *The Fifth Discipline*. Cambridge, MA: MIT Press.

Shaw, M. E. (1976) *Group Dynamics: The Psychology of Small Groups* (2nd edn). New York: McGraw-Hill.

Shea, M. (1993) *Personal Impact, Presence, Para-Language and the Art of Good Communication*. London: Sinclair-Stevenson.

Siraj-Blatchford, I. and Clark, P. (2000) *Supporting Identity, Diversity and Language in the Early Years*. Buckingham: Open University Press.

Siraj-Blatchford, I. and Manni, L. (2007) *Effective Leadership in the Early Years Sector: The ELEYS Study*. London: Institute of Education, University of London.

Siraj-Blatchford, I., Sylva, K., Muttock, S., Gilden, R. and Bell, D. (2002) *Researching Effective Pedagogy in the Early Years (REPEY)*. DfES Research Report 356, London: DfES/HMSO.

Smith, A. and Langston, A. (1999) *Managing Staff in Early Years Settings*. London: Routledge.

Solley, K. (2003) What do early childhood leaders do to maintain and enhance the significance of the early years? Paper presented at the Institute of Education, University of London, 22 May, available at www.early-education.org.uk/resources/wdeyl95.doc (accessed 16 November 2007).

Southworth, G. (2004) *Primary School Leadership in Context: Leading Small, Medium and Large Sized Schools*. London: RoutledgeFalmer.

Stephenson, J. and Sampson, J. (1994) Conditions for effective mentoring within the school. In Yeomans, R. and Sampson, J. (eds) *Mentorship in the Primary School*. London: Falmer Press.

Stipek, D. and Ogana, T. (2000) *Early Childhood Education*. Los Angeles: University of California, Los Angeles Center for Healthier Children, Families and Communities.

Stogdill, R. M. (1948) Personal factors associated with leadership. a survey of the literature. *Journal of Psychology*, 25: 35–71.

Sure Start Keighley (2005) *Evaluation Report Summary* (one of three evaluations commissioned by Sure Start Keighley and carried out by Leeds University). Keighley: Sure Start Keighley.

Sutherland, M. (2005) *Gifted and Talented in the Early Years*. London: Sage/Paul Chapman.

Sylva, K., Melhuish, E. C., Sammons, P., Siraj-Blatchford, I. and Taggart, B. (2004) *The Effective Provision of Pre-School Education (EPPE) Project: Final Report*. London: DfEE/Institute of Education, University of London.

Sylva, K., Siraj-Blatchford, I., Melhuish, E. C., Lewis, K., Morahan, M. and Sadler, S. (1999) *The Effective Provision of Pre-School Education (EPPE) Project: Technical Paper 6A – Characteristics of pre-school environments*. London: DfEE/Institute of Education, University of London.

Sylva, K., Taggart, B., Siraj-Blatchford, I., Totsika, V., Ereky-Stevens, K., Gilden, R. and Bell, D. (2007) Curricular quality and day-to-day learning activities in pre-school. *International Journal of Early Years Education*, 15 (1): 49–65.

Tovey, H. (2007) *Playing Outdoors: Spaces and Places Risk and Challenge*. Maidenhead: Open University Press.

Trevarthen, C. (2001) Intrinsic motives for companionship in understanding their origin, development and significance for mental health. *Infant Mental Health Journal*, 22 (1–2): 95–131.

Trodd, L. (2005) Launching into learning: becoming a reflective practitioner. In Dryden, L., Forbes, R., Mukherji, P., Pound, L., Joshi, U., Chawla-Duggan, R., Menon, C. and Trodd, L. *Essential Early Years*. London: Hodder Arnold.

Tuckman, B. W. (1965) Developmental sequence in small groups. *Psychological Bulletin*, 63: 384–99.

Tuckman, B. W. and Jensen, M. A. (1977) Stages of small group development revisited. *Group and Organisational Studies*, 2: 419–27.

United Nations Children's Fund (UNICEF) (2007) *Child Poverty in Perspective: An Overview of Child Well-being in Rich Countries*. Report Card 7, Innocenti Research Centre, Florence, Italy: UNICEF.

Valentine, M. (2006) *The Reggio Emilia Approach to Early Years Education*. Dundee: Scottish Consultative Council on the Curriculum.

Vygotsky, L. (1978) *Mind in Society*. Cambridge, MA: Harvard University Press.

Walden, D. and Shiba, S. (2001) *Four Practical Revolutions in Management Systems for Creating Organisational Capabilities* (2nd edn). New York: Productivity Press.

Wall, K. (2006) *Special Needs and Early Years: A Practitioner's Guide* (2nd edn). London: Paul Chapman.

Waniganayake, M. (2006) Preface. to Rodd, J. *Leadership in Early Childhood*. Maidenhead: Open University Press.

Warin, J. (2007) Joined-Up services for young children and their families: papering over the cracks or re-constructing the foundations? *Children and Society*, 21: 87–97.

West, M. A. (2004) *Effective Team Work: Practical Lessons from Organisational Research* (2nd edn). Oxford: BPS Blackwell.

Whalley, M. (2002) Creative waves: National College of School Leadership discussion paper on future schools. Keynote address at British Educational Research Association Annual Conference, 2002, available at http://www.ncsl.org.uk/media/F7B/95/randd-futures-creative-waves.pdf (acessed 31 October 2007).

Whalley, M. (2005a) Developing leadership approaches for early years settings. Pen Green: unpublished lecture, available at www.ncsl.org.uk/media/F58/76/communityleadership-together-m-whalley.ppt (accessed 30 November 2007).

Whalley, M. (2005b) Leadership professional development for integrated services. Unpublished keynote address for Daycare Trust Annual Conference, 2005, available at www.daycaretrust.org.uk/mod/fileman/files/Margy_Whalley_web_version.ppt (accessed 7 December 2007).

Whalley, M. and the Pen Green Centre Team (2007) *Involving Parents in Their Children's Learning* (2nd edn). London: Paul Chapman.

Whitaker, P. (2004) *NPQICL Pedagogical Leadership*. Nottingham: NCSL.

Whitebread, D. (2003) Young children learning and early years teaching. In Whitebread, D. (ed.) *Teaching and Learning in the Early Years* (2nd edn). London: RoutledgeFalmer.

Willan, J. (2007) Research projects in early childhood studies: students' active explorations of children's worlds. In Willan, J., Parker-Rees, R. and Savage, J. *Early Childhood Studies* (2nd edition). Exeter: Learning Matters.

Williams, H. (1996) *Managing Groups and Teams*. Hemel Hempstead: Prentice-Hall.

Wilmot, E. (2006) *Personalising Learning in the Primary Classroom*. Carmarthen: Crown House Publishing.

Wood, E. and Attfield, J. (2005) *Play, Learning and the Early Childhood Curriculum* (2nd edn). London: Sage.

Wright, P. (1996) *Managerial Leadership*. London: Routledge.

Yukl, G. (1989) Managerial leadership: a review of theory and research. *Journal of Management*, 15 (2): 251–89. University of London

Index